# VICTORIAN FURNITURE

Styles and Prices

by

Robert W. and Harriett Swedberg

New Revised Edition

Photographs: by the authors
Printing and Enlarging: Tom Luse

**1876 and 1979 Prices**

Photographs: by the authors
Printing and Enlarging: Tom Luse

# Dedication

As great as is our love and appreciation of antiques, it could never be greater than for the two boys, Adam and Cody, to whom we affectionately dedicate this book.

ISBN 0-87069-265-8
Library of Congress # 76-6832

Cover photography by Edward J. Stanek

Published by

Wallace-Homestead Book Co.
1912 Grand Avenue
Des Moines, Iowa 50305

# Generalized Statements Regarding Prices — 1979

### Assets which tend to add dollars

- marble tops
- sets—chairs, bedroom, parlor and dining suites
- oval and curved shapes
- ornate lines—carving, pierced or applied designs
- rosewood
- wishbone mirrors
- versatility—pieces which can be used almost anywhere
- miniatures—children's or doll sizes

### Characteristics which tend to lack appreciation

- single chairs
- rectangular lines
- gauche designs
- single purpose pieces
- wooden tops
- uncomfortable chairs, sofas

Why do some prices accelerate while others remain stable? Supply and demand is a major factor while style requires consideration.

Ponder on parlor tables. Many seek marble tops rather than wooden versions and, generally speaking, there seems to be a preference for lighter toned stone over the dark hues. Currently, oval tops outsell the rectilinear, so one would expect to find oval marble top tables escalated in price while those of wood with rectangular lines remain about the same. In a similar vein, marble on chests, commodes, sideboards and hall trees, resembles the *a la mode* on pies as an added attraction.

Sets seem to sell well. Single chairs have a lesser value when compared to matching sets. In parlor furnishings, some enjoy a sofa, lady's and gentleman's chair or perhaps a few side chairs which share the same pattern. Dining room and bedroom suites are quite desirable. Comfort, too, is a consideration.

An Englishman who designed furniture, Charles Lock Eastlake, felt square lines had a dual advantage in that it combined to save wood and provide added structural strength. In 1868, he published a book showing box-type furniture, and the idea spread to the United States (circa 1870-1890s) where many unnecessary machine-made do-dads (which Eastlake disliked) were added. At present, Eastlake's squares and rectangles are not fervently finding favor, and therefore their selling tags have stabilized.

Rosewood is an exotic wood and commands a higher price than the more commonly available walnut of the Victorian era. Wishbone mirrors, swinging framed looking glasses in U shaped decorative supports are sought on chests and bureaus.

Versatile pieces have a priority rating. The small common washstand can be an end table, a bedside or bathroom stand or a hall accessory. A bureau commode's storage unit and dainty size lends itself well to use almost anywhere which retains its popularity.

Women adore irresistible tiny tot furniture of days gone by. A cradle, pint-sized bed, table, petite rocker, or a child's high chair attract attention and many doll collectors delight in finding tiny furnishings. Nostalgia causes some families to keep possessions of little ones. "All the Huntington babies slept in this cradle" or "this was my grandpa's high chair" are statements said with sentimental pride as the proper piece is fondly displayed. A large chair could be parted with, but not the child's rocker which the familial young ones can still enjoy. The result is fewer miniature articles available for resale causing the prices to ascend.

These factors were considered when price advances were analyzed and the upward trend is reflected in the 1979 listing.

# Acknowledgments

The authors would like to sincerely thank the following individuals and dealers who so unselfishly gave of their time and knowledge in assisting us to obtain photographs and prices for this book. A thanks, too, to the many individuals and dealers who did not wish to be named.

Mrs. Mary Baker

Banowetz Antiques, Maquoketa, Iowa

Barney's Island Antiques, Naples, Florida

Carl Blade

Frederick and Elizabeth Brinkmeyer, St. Louis, Missouri

Busvan, San Francisco, California

The Church Mouse, Port Byron, Illinois

Pauline Coady

Jack and Till Cummins

Kathryn Craig Antiques, Kewanee, Illinois

Ted and Barbara Davies

Dot's Antiques and Upholstery Shop, East Amhurst, New York

Adam, Cody, and Karen Elvidge

Eurasian Antiques, Honolulu, Hawaii

Leigh and Andrée Fiedler

Jerry and Mary Fisher

Eugene and Earlene Fowler

Just and Olive Frizol

Rodney and Dorothea Fryxell

Dale Fugate, Austin, Texas

Gates Antiques Ltd., Midlothian, Virginia

The Golden Eagle Antiques, Inc., Tampa, Florida

Grace's Antiques, Evansville, Indiana

Karl and Sigrid Haytcher

Honest Jon's Antiques, Salt Lake City, Utah

Hoosier Heritage Antiques, Fort Wayne, Indiana

Hudson's Antiques and Auction, Tanner, Alabama

Ellen J. Jenkins

Lena's Antiques, Richmond, Kentucky

Bill and Fern Lyon

Mrs. Grant McGill

Marshall's Antiques, Augusta, Maine

The Mill Antiques, Woodruff, Wisconsin

Ethel Myers

John and Elizabeth Noonan

The Nostalgia Shop, Buffalo, Illinois

The Outpost, Aledo, Illinois

Ann Parsons

Herbert and Delta Parsons

Martha Parsons

Michael and Marilyn Payne

Mary Rachael Antiques, Washington, Illinois

Red's Antiques, Union Bridge, Maryland

Ricklef's Woodwork Shop, Anamosa, Iowa

The Stable on the Alley, Cedar Rapids, Iowa

Stubblefield Antiques, Eaton, Ohio

Thompson's House of Antiques, Columbus, Ohio

Elizabeth Towler Antiques, Elkins, West Virginia

Mike and Coleen Tracy

The Trading Post, Aledo, Illinois

The Wayside Shop, Wilmington, Illinois

Tim and Paula Ziegler

# Table of Contents

# Chapter I
## A Guide to Prices

The determination of prices was the major task which confronted us in compiling this book, for we felt that they should as validly and accurately as possible represent what dealers throughout the country were asking for particular articles of furniture. In order to accomplish this purpose, we prepared a six page questionnaire, listed articles of Victorian furniture by room, briefly described them, and then sent them to over 200 dealers in all parts of the country. The response was indeed gratifying for we received samplings from such states as California, Hawaii, Utah, Indiana, Iowa, Illinois, Ohio, Wisconsin, Tennessee, Kentucky, Alabama, Florida, West Virginia, Virginia, Maryland, New York, and Maine.

Because the questionnaire had to be as brief as possible to avoid a time hardship on the cooperating dealers, we asked them to give a price range for the individual pieces. We felt that this price range would reflect differences in style and construction, condition, and the local supply and demand. An average price, as most price books state, would not reveal these differences.

Assuredly it was not an easy task for these cooperating dealers to complete the questionnaire, for when you are given a description such as "hall tree with mirror, marble insert, and umbrella holders" many mental pictures enter the mind. The visual memories could well range from the very simple, straight line style with small mirror to a very ornately carved and decorated hall tree with a large mirror. Therefore, the price ranges in the summary are great in many cases.

In addition to the questionnaires, prices were derived from auctions and estate sales, dealer advertisements in trade magazines, and at antique shows. All of the data from these sources was used to complete the **Walnut Victorian Price Guide Summary** that follows this section.

Certainly, in addition to style and construction and regional differences, the condition of the article is a price factor. Its roughness can often bring the price near the lower level if one considers the amount of work necessary to renovate it. Some of these factors may include:

1. missing or replaced hardware
2. a warped, split or badly stained top
3. badly worn or broken drawer runners and slides
4. broken or missing chair rungs
5. broken or missing cane from chairs or rockers
6. broken mirrors or those in which the silver has cracked
7. broken, missing or replaced marble
8. loose legs on chairs or sofas
9. the condition of the upholstery
10. the finish on the piece may be alligatored or painted

So, unless you are handy at refinishing and restoration, it may be unwise to buy a piece that needs extensive repair, for your total cost may exceed what you would spend buying a comparable style in mint condition.

The prices listed under the pictures in the body of the book represent a variation, too, in that the prices vary according to what section of the country they are found. Let the readers be assured that the prices, though as accurate and valid as could be achieved, represent no absolutes, and do not, of course, show every type of Victorian furniture manufactured.

The price summary guide that follows is similar in format to the questionnaires on which the prices in this book are primarily based.

# Walnut Victorian Furniture Price Guide Summary

This summary retains prices from the original survey.

| Room Location and Description of Furniture | Price Range |
|---|---|

**A. Hall**

1. Hall trees (stands) with:
   - a. mirror and umbrella holders .............................. $175.00 - 400.00
   - b. mirror and marble insert ................................ 145.00 - 450.00
   - c. mirror, marble insert, umbrella holders, and hat hooks ...... 295.00 - 750.00
2. Pier mirrors ................................................. 190.00 - 750.00
3. Hat racks (folding or solid) ................................. 45.00 - 175.00

**B. Library - Parlor**

1. Chairs
   - a. side chair with upholstered seat and back ................. 75.00 - 250.00
   - b. side chair with upholstered seat and fruit flower carved wooden back ................................................ 65.00 - 350.00
   - c. side chair with upholstered seat and finger roll back ....... 65.00 - 275.00
   - d. side chair with machine lines and carving, upholstered seat and back (Eastlake) .......................................... 65.00 - 250.00
   - e. arm chair, Louis XV or Renaissance substyle .............. 125.00 - 285.00
   - f. arm chair with machine lines and carving, upholstered seat and back (Eastlake) ........................................ 65.00 - 275.00
   - g. lady's chair ............................................. 175.00 - 400.00
   - h. gentleman's chair ....................................... 175.00 - 485.00
2. Rockers
   - a. cane seat and back (lady's or slipper) ................... 95.00 - 325.00
   - b. cane seat and back (gentleman's type) ................... 85.00 - 400.00
   - c. cane seat with wooden designed back (original cane may be covered with upholstery or needle point) ................... 75.00 - 175.00
   - d. upholstered seat and back (Lincoln type) ................. 100.00 - 450.00
   - e. folding fire side ....................................... 35.00 - 175.00
   - f. platform ............................................... 75.00 - 300.00
3. Desks
   - a. cylinder front secretary ................................ 475.00 - 1,500.00
   - b. lady's cylinder front desk .............................. 500.00 - 1,200.00
   - c. two piece secretary bookcase with fold out writing surface ... 250.00 - 1,500.00
   - d. slant front secretary ................................... 300.00 - 1,800.00
   - e. plantation, two pieces .................................. 350.00 - 1,200.00
   - f. two piece on legs with wooden drop front in top section (Lincoln type) ............................................ 225.00 - 895.00
   - g. lady's ................................................. 175.00 - 750.00
   - h. Davenport (with side drawers) .......................... 350.00 - 850.00
   - i. bureau ................................................. 300.00 - 750.00
   - j. bureau with bookcase ................................... 495.00 - 1,500.00
   - k. table desk (office table) ............................... 175.00 - 450.00
   - l. lift lid (schoolmaster's type) ........................... 250.00 - 600.00
   - m. drop lid with doors or drawers below ................... 300.00 - 600.00
4. Whatnots (etagères)
   - a. corner with 4 or 5 graduated shelves ................... 85.00 - 275.00
   - b. flush to wall with 4 or 5 graduated shelves .............. 85.00 - 350.00
   - c. hanging (corner or flush) .............................. 40.00 - 275.00

      d. hanging with glass doors and shelves ..................... 75.00 - 300.00

      e. etagère with marble, mirror and shelves ................... 495.00 - 1,600.00

5. Tables

      a. turtle top, wooden ...................................... 100.00 - 350.00

      b. oval top, wooden ....................................... 100.00 - 350.00

      c. rectangular or square top, wooden ....................... 65.00 - 450.00

      d. card or game table ...................................... 150.00 - 400.00

      e. tilt top, pedestal base .................................. 125.00 - 500.00

      f. round or oval (rosewood) ............................... 500.00 - 600.00

      g. round game table, wooden .............................. 175.00 - 350.00

      h. library, wooden ........................................ 200.00 - 600.00

      i. turtle top, marble ...................................... 250.00 - 675.00

      j. oval top, marble ....................................... 150.00 - 450.00

      k. oval top, marble with carved animal figures near base ....... 200.00 - 850.00

      l. rectangular or square top, marble ...................... 125.00 - 450.00

6. Sofas - Settees - Loveseats

      a. medallion, cameo, mirror back ......................... 300.00 - 1,000.00

      b. serpentine back with carved crest....................... 225.00 - 1,200.00

      c. finger roll back ........................................ 250.00 - 800.00

      d. carved crest (sometimes removeable) ................... 185.00 - 700.00

      e. upholstered back framed in wooden designed panels ....... 195.00 - 900.00

      f. Eastlake style ......................................... 200.00 - 475.00

7. Stands (candle, plant, Bible)

      a. round marble insert .................................... 125.00 - 250.00

      b. rectangular marble top ................................. 150.00 - 275.00

      c. round wooden top ..................................... 75.00 - 175.00

      d. square wooden top .................................... 65.00 - 150.00

C. Dining Room

1. Tables

      a. drop leaf, rectangular or square (4 legs) ................. 85.00 - 450.00

      b. drop leaf, oval (4 legs) ................................. 100.00 - 350.00

      c. extension, rectangular or square (4 legs) ................. 115.00 - 450.00

      d. extension, oval (4 legs) ................................ 135.00 - 350.00

      e. gate leg (2 additional legs support the leaves when they are raised) ................................................ 125.00 - 500.00

      f. round extension, pedestal base .......................... 450.00 - 750.00

      g. square extension, pedestal base......................... 400.00 - 600.00

2. Bookcases (cupboards) ...................................... 225.00 - 1,500.00

3. Sideboards (buffets) ....................................... 250.00 - 2,500.00

4. Chairs

      a. arm ................................................. 65.00 - 150.00

      b. cane seat, plain back, demi-arms ....................... 50.00 - 125.00

      c. cane seat, fancy back, demi-arms ....................... 65.00 - 150.00

      d. cane seat without demi-arms ........................... 35.00 - 100.00

D. Bedroom

1. Stands (wooden top)

      a. common washstand (towel bars, one drawer and shelf below) . 95.00 - 275.00

      b. toilet stand (one or two drawers, no shelf) ................. 75.00 - 200.00

      c. toilet stand (one drawer and shelf) ...................... 75.00 - 250.00

      d. lamp stand, usually square (one drawer) ................. 65.00 - 150.00

e.  sewing stand with drop leaves ........................... 125.00 – 300.00

f.  sewing stand with one or two drawers and shelf ............ 65.00 – 225.00

2.  Commode washstands (drawers and doors)

   a. marble top with pull out towel bar ...................... 175.00 – 495.00

   b. marble top with one door and three or four drawers ........ 195.00 – 465.00

   c. marble top with two doors and one or two drawers (no splash back) ....................................................... 200.00 – 450.00

   d. marble top with two doors and one or two drawers (with splash back and soap shelves) ........................... 200.00 – 600.00

   e. wooden top with two doors and one drawer .............. 150.00 – 350.00

   f. wooden top with one door and three drawers .............. 75.00 – 395.00

   g. lift top with two doors below ......................... 175.00 – 350.00

3.  Bureau washstand (three drawers or four if top two are small)

   a. wooden top ........................................ 150.00 – 395.00

   b. marble top ........................................ 175.00 – 400.00

   c. wooden top with towel bars .......................... 75.00 – 300.00

4.  Dressers (bureaus or dressing cases)

   a. wooden top with swing mirror and handkerchief boxes ....... 175.00 – 400.00

   b. wooden top with no mirror but with handkerchief boxes ...... 125.00 – 350.00

   c. wooden top with wishbone mirror and handkerchief boxes ... 185.00 – 650.00

   d. wooden top with no mirror and no handkerchief boxes ....... 175.00 – 350.00

   e. wooden top with drop well or step down, tall attached mirror and two lower drawers ................................. 225.00 – 600.00

   f. marble top with swing mirror and handkerchief boxes ....... 200.00 – 600.00

   g. marble top with no mirror and no handkerchief boxes ........ 200.00 – 450.00

   h. marble top with swing mirror and no handkerchief boxes ..... 350.00 – 850.00

   i. marble insert with swing mirror and handkerchief boxes ..... 175.00 – 450.00

   j. marble insert with no mirror but with handkerchief boxes .... 150.00 – 350.00

   k. marble top with drop well or step down, tall attached mirror and two lower drawers ................................. 350.00 – 850.00

   l. five or six drawer chiffonier ............................ 300.00 – 500.00

   m. three piece bedroom suits ...........................1,500.00 – 4,000.00

5.  Wardrobes (armoires) ................................. 250.00 – 2,500.00

6.  Bedsteads

   a. spool (Jenny Lind) ................................. 145.00 – 650.00

   b. rope ............................................. 150.00 – 350.00

   c. hired hand, day bed, window seat ..................... 175.00 – 450.00

   d. tester or canopy .................................. 450.00 – 2,500.00

   e. high back (7' or higher) with burled and carved decorations .. 400.00 – 1,500.00

   f. high back (under 7') with burled and carved decorations ..... 250.00 – 900.00

7.  Chaise longue ....................................... 150.00 – 750.00

8.  Mirrors ...............................................

   a. cheval ........................................... 150.00 – 500.00

   b. dressing stand (portable) ............................ 95.00 – 275.00

9.  Racks

   a. clothes (valet) .................................... 75.00 – 250.00

   b. blanket .......................................... 75.00 – 150.00

   c. towel ............................................ 40.00 – 125.00

E. Nursery
   1. Cradles
      a. swinging (on base) ............................... 150.00 - 550.00
      b. spindle (on rockers) ............................. 145.00 - 450.00
      c. slats or solid .................................. 150.00 - 300.00
   2. Baby bed ......................................... 135.00 - 350.00
   3. Youth bed ........................................ 150.00 - 450.00
   4. Rockers .......................................... 175.00 - 295.00
   5. High chairs ...................................... 75.00 - 185.00

# 1876 Prices

In compiling current costs we thought it might be intriguing and eye opening to antique dealers, collectors, and other interested persons to learn the prices of furniture that were prevalent when our country was one hundred years old. To achieve this goal we researched prices from newspapers, magazines, and catalogs of that period and have included some of the information from the magazines and newspapers within the various sections of this book. However, the main body of price data, taken from the 1873 and 1876 catalogs (with photographs and prices) of the Nelson, Matter & Co., Manufacturers of Furniture, Grand Rapids, Michigan, is included in the summary that follows. Terms used in the identifications are taken directly from the catalogs, and the readers will note that in many instances they differ from our present day labeling. Also to be observed is the fact that there are many examples of furniture that could be purchased either in an unfinished or a finished state. Many factors account for the variance of prices as are listed below:

1. extent of burl veneering, engraving, carving, and decorations added for style differences
2. sizes of plates (mirrors) and toilets (mirror frames)
3. sizes of marble tops
4. height of marble splash backs
5. type of handles used—wooden carved or ebony gilt drop pulls
6. height of bedsteads, hall stands, bookcases, and sideboards
7. the inclusion of slipper drawers (secret drawers at the base of bureau) or secret drawers or compartments
8. the inclusion of boxes or decks (handkerchief drawers)
9. top dimensions of parlor tables, dining tables, desks, library tables, and stands
10. whether the top is wooden or marble
11. width of sideboards and dressing cases (drop well dressers)

## 1876 Walnut Victorian Price Guide Summary

| Description of Furniture | Unfinished | Finished |
|---|---|---|
| **Hall Stands (Trees)** | | |
| 1. With mirrors, umbrella holders, and marble— height: 7 ft., 3 in. to 7 ft., 6 in.; plate (mirror) size: 10 in. x 12 in. to 18 in. x 36 in. | $ 7.50 - 25.00 | $10.00 - 34.00 |
| **Desks** | | |
| 1. Secretary (slant front with bookcase) with doors or drawers below—height: 8 ft., 2 in. to 8 ft., 7 in.; width: 3 ft., 3 in to 4 ft., 2 in. | 27.00 - 45.00 | 37.00 - 55.00 |

2. Enameled cloth top office table with two drawers—
width: 46 in. to 58 in. ..........................     10.00 - 13.00

3. Ladies' parlor desk, veneered, three drawers in the
end (Davenport type) ........................ 16.00 - 18.50    20.00 - 23.00

4. Fall leaf desk, two drawers with table (Lincoln type) 10.00    12.00

5. Business desk, hinged cornice, two doors in upper
section, two shelves in upper middle, two drawers
below, carved handles, and turned legs—width: 4
ft., 2 in. .................................... 28.00    32.00

6. Parlor desk, burled veneer, drop slant front, one
long drawer, two doors or drawers below, shelf at
top ....................................... 42.00   43.00

## Whatnots

1. Corner or side, five shelves, bracket or turned
standards, with or without fret at the rear of the
shelves ...................................... 2.25 - 6.00    3.00 - 7.50

## Wood Top Centre Tables

1. Serpentine top, beveled corner, engraved legs—top:
21 in. x 27 in. .............................. 4.50    5.50

2. Oval top—top: 18 in. x 24 in. to 24 in. x 32 in. ....... 4.00 - 6.50    5.00 - 8.00

3. Rectangular top, beveled corner—top: 18 in. x 25½
in. to 20 in. x 28½ in. ........................... 4.00 - 6.00    6.00 - 9.00

4. Library table, burled and veneered—top: 26 in. x
46 in. to 27 in. x 52 in. ....................... 28.00 - 30.00    36.00 - 40.00

## Marble Top Centre Tables

1. Serpentine top, beveled corner, engraved legs—top:
21 in. x 27 in. .............................. 9.50    10.25

2. Oval top—top: 18 in. x 24 in. to 24 in. x 32 in. ..... 7.50 - 16.00    8.50 - 18.50

3. Rectangular top, beveled corner—top: 18 in. x 25½
in. to 20 in. x 28½ in. ......................... 8.00 - 10.50    9.50 - 13.00

## Couch Frames

1. Fine veneered (not upholstered) ................. 7.00 - 8.00    9.00 - 10.00

2. Enameled veneers, walnut moulded (not uphol-
stered) ...................................... 4.00 - 4.50    5.00 - 5.50

3. Above frames upholstered with:
a) tapestry Brussels carpet
b) union terry plain
c) all wool terry plain
d) all wool puffed front    11.50 - 13.00

## Foot Rest Frames

1. Burl veneered with slipper box ................. 4.00    5.00

## Bible Stands

1. Fancy, recessed top—marble: 12 in. x 12 in. ...... 5.00    6.00

2. Fancy, round top—marble: 15 in. x 15 in. ........ 6.00    7.00

## Tables

1. Fall leaf dining table, patent extension frame—top:
42 in. x 56 in. to 48 in. x 56 in. (ash or cherry) ...... 5.00 - 5.50    5.50 - 6.00

2. Breakfast—3 ft., 3¼ ft, 3½ ft. and 3¾ ft. (ash or
cherry) ..................................... 1.00 per foot    1.15 per foot

3. Round table—3 foot (ash or cherry) ............. 1.00 per foot    1.15 per foot

4. Extension table made to size (walnut) ........... 1.20 per foot    1.30 per foot

5. Fall leaves ...................................... 1.00 each

## Bookcases

1. Two drawers below, two large glass doors above, ebony and gilt drop pulls—width: 4 ft; height: 6 ft., 5 in. .................................... 20.00       28.00
2. Two drawers below, two large glass doors above, ebony and gilt drop pulls—width: 4 ft., 6 in.; height: 9 ft. ................................. 40.00       48.00

## Sideboards

1. Burl veneered panels, marble, two drawers, two doors below—marble top: 19 in. x 42 in. to 21 in. x 60 in.; height: 7 ft., 4 in. to 8 ft., 6 in.; plate (mirror): 14 in. x 24 in. to 18 in. x 30 in. .......... 29.00 - 77.00       36.00 - 90.00

## Stands (wood top)

1. Lamp stand, one drawer, square top: 18 in. x 18 in. (no shelf) ..................... 1.25       1.50
2. Toilet Stand, one drawer (no shelf): 18 in. x 30 in. (top) ........................ 1.50       1.90
3. Common washstand, one drawer and shelf: 16 in. x 20 in. (top) ..................... 2.00       2.40
4. Common washstand, one drawer and shelf: 16 in. x 28 in. (top) ..................... 2.25       2.75
5. Fancy pillar, scalloped or round top: 21 in. x 21 in.    1.75       2.25
6. Round top, fancy pillar—top: 30 in. x 30 in. to 36 in. x 36 in. ...................................... 3.00 - 3.50       3.50 - 4.25

## Commode Washstands (doors and drawers)

1. Marble, low or high splash backs, veneered, paneled, carved ........................... 14.00 - 21.00       16.00 - 24.00
2. Wooden top, plain, moulded front, enameled veneers .................................... 4.25 - 5.25       5.25 - 7.75

## Three Drawer Bureau Washstands

1. Wooden top, plain, with towel bars at ends ....... 4.50       5.25
2. Wooden top, plain, moulded front, or enameled veneers .................................... 5.25 - 6.00       6.00 - 7.00
3. Numbers one and two above in ash ............. 3.75 - 5.25       5.50 - 6.25
4. Numbers one and two above in walnut stained ends    4.25 - 5.75       5.00 - 6.75

## Bureaus Without Toilets (Dressers without mirrors)

1. Three or four drawers, wooden top, plain or moulded front, decks or no decks (handkerchief boxes) ..................................... 6.50 - 8.25       8.00 - 10.00

## Bureaus With Toilets (dressers with mirrors)

1. Three or four drawers, wooden top, two decks or two boxes, plain or veneered—toilet size: 13 in. x 22 in. to 16 in. x 28 in. ........................ 10.50 - 13.00       15.00 - 18.00

## Bedsteads

1. Veneering, carving, and turning—height: 5 ft., 4 in. to 6 ft., 9 in. ............................. 5.50 - 10.00       7.00 - 13.00
2. Veneering, carving, and turning—height: 7 ft., 1 in. to 8 ft., 3 in. ............................. 14.00 - 45.00       19.00 - 57.00
3. Fancy veneering, carving, and turning—height: 8 ft. ..................................... 80.00       100.00
4. Rich and elegant designed carving, veneering, and turning—height: 9 ft. 8 in. ....................130.00       150.00

**Towel Racks**
1. Plain or fancy, walnut or ash . . . . . . . . . . . . . . . . . . . .     .56 - 1.75          .75 - 2.00

**Cribs (cradles)**
1. Square with small posts, spindle turned or round
   cornered (maple) . . . . . . . . . . . . . . . . . . . . . . . . . . . . .     1.50 - 2.00         2.00 - 2.50
2. Same as number one above but in walnut . . . . . . . .     2.50               3.00

**Cribs (Baby beds)**
1. Single, spindle side, paneled—29 in. x 54 in.  . . . . . .     4.25               5.00
2. Double, spindle side, paneled—37 in. x 54 in. . . . . . .     4.25               5.00

**Chamber Suits Embracing Three Pieces [Bureau, Washstand, and Bedstead] ***

|   | Bedstead Height | Plate Size | Finished in Ash | Walnut |
|---|---|---|---|---|
| 1. Wooden tops | 4 ft. 6 in. to 6 ft. 10 in. | 12 in. x 20 in. to 18 in. x 30 in. | 23.75 - 46.75 | 27.50 - 51.00 |
| 2. Marble tops | 5 ft., 7 in. to 7 ft., 8 in. | 14 in. x 14 in. to 18 in. x 36 in. | 47.00 - 85.50 | 51.00 - 94.50 |
| 3. Marble tops | 7 ft., 6 in. to 7 ft., 8 in. | 18 in. x 36 in. to 20 in. x 48 in. | not made | 105.00 - 170.00 |

*More expensive suits had dressing cases rather than bureaus.

**Dressing Case**
1. Two lower drawers with two small drawers at each
   side of drop well—toilet size: 18 in. x 40 in. to 22 in.
   x 54 in. . . . . . . . . . . . . . . . . . . . . . . . . . . . . . . . . .     30.50 - 79.00       36.50 - 92.00

**Dressing Case Suit**
1. This is a rich and elegant design. The dressing case
   has two secret jewelry drawers. There are nine
   drawers in the case, and three locks secure them
   all. The bed is 9 ft., 8 in. high with 5 ft. slats. The
   toilet on the case is 28 in. x 64 in. A somnoe (a one
   drawer, one door washstand) is the third piece. . . .320.00                 370.00

**Marble Top Bureaus with toilets**  . . . . . . . . . . . . . . . . . . . .                           23.75 - 59.50
   **(dressers with mirrors)**
1. Three or four drawers, marble top, two decks or
   two boxes, plain or veneered, slipper drawer,
   projection front, drop pulls, carved pulls, toilet size
   14 in. x 24 in. to 18 in. x 40 in.  . . . . . . . . . . . . . . . . .     18.75 - 46.50       23.75 - 59.50

# Chapter 2
## The Victorian Age

Antique black walnut furniture? Those four words symbolize money. Antiques are considered one of the seven best investments in the world today with silver, furniture, and jewelry leading. So greedy are some unscrupulous people for expensive walnut lumber which can be sliced into thirty two sheets per inch to make veneers that surreptitiously they are cutting down trees in other's yards and hauling them away without bothering to receive the owner's permission. In this day of pressed wood or formica construction, the thick walnut in furniture of yore comes forth with a solid citizen status.

Back in the mid-nineteenth century when Grand Rapids, Michigan, was the furniture capital of America, the adjacent area was verdant with trees. During the winter enough black walnut, cherry, white ash, basswood, red oak, elm, beech, hickory, or hard maple might be pulled overland from the snowclad forests in bobsleds in a few weeks' time to supply a leading furniture making company with enough lumber to last an entire year.

Then came the day that people who advocated conservation anticipated and dreaded. In the 1880's black walnut became very scarce and could no longer be chopped hit and miss from the forests. At a time when England's Queen Victoria was growing old and her vitality was eroding away, the "age of walnut" named for her was waning too.

Victoria, charming, yet sometimes difficult and enigmatic, assumed the imposing title Queen of the United Kingdom of Great Britain and Ireland and Empress of India at the age of eighteen. She ruled from 1837 to 1901, longer than any other British monarch. The time spanning her reign is known as the Victorian Era, and furniture produced then is called by her name. While styles changed during those years from the heavy imposing handmade mahogany Empire, circa 1810-1840, which was fading out as she ascended the throne, to the rectangular lines of Eastlake (1870's), most people remember that the switch from made-at-home by hand to products produced by power driven machines in factories occurred in the nineteenth century.

Many stereotype the flowing elliptical lines of Louis XV with rococo designs and the elaborate, overly ornate, carved Renaissance Revival pieces as Victorian furniture. Woods on the most wanted list were walnut, mahogany, and rosewood. The latter two, with their reddish tones, had to be imported, and rosewood with its dark lines sometimes even smelled "mighty Lak a rose". While furniture constructed from imported lumber rather than from trees which might grow profusely on ones own "back forty" farm acreage seemed exotic, walnut was utilized more than the other two during the mid-Victorian "Age of Walnut". It was more plentiful, easily available, and less expensive: quite a contrast to its station today. Generally, cabinetmakers stained walnut a reddish hue to make it resemble mahogany which was considered the affleunt wood.

Since Victorians enjoyed "going creative" as they borrowed indiscriminately from the past and combined unrelated patterns, diversified furniture emerged. For example, why not feature twisting legs? Lathes for making turnings were known from ancient times, but apprentices no longer had to manipulate them by hand because steam provided the necessary power. The new gauge lathe could produce more in one day than three men working by hand, so turnings could be present in profusion on legs, pilasters, or railings. Previously, cabinetmakers consulted directly with clients and knew their preferences as they crafted objects to order. With machines, furnishings were mass produced and were made available for anyone to purchase.

This shift from home to factory encompassed scores of years, and there were still craftsmen in rural areas who pursued their trade late in the century just as there are "do-it-yourselfers" currently who enjoy making pieces of furniture with home tools. Also, style changes took awhile to be absorbed, and there were transitional pieces which incorporated a little of the old with the new so that they are not pure examples of either form. How much easier it would be to classify furniture if one type terminated abruptly and another emerged immediately. Instead, styles ran concurrently.

Actually, the separation of Victorian trends into early, mid, and late has arbitrary dividing lines. Some authors include American Empire but this can stand alone as a distinct style and time. Some place Louis XV under early, but since its lines seem to flow naturally into the ornate Renaissance Revival, it is listed here as a middle style. Because some types lasted longer than others, it's difficult to decide on a classification which places them in one category when their influence prevails for many years.

The following chart considers dates averaged through examination of various sources since discrepancies occur in research materials. As an example, one authority will designate machined spool furniture as an 1850's popular speciality. Another may mention the 1820's while a third may suggest an 1830 date. Therefore, generalizations become a necessity.

# The Victorian Age

### Early Victorian 1837-1840's

| Name of Style | Dates | Characteristics | Wood |
|---|---|---|---|
| Spool Furniture | 1820-1870 | While most of the heavy, imposing Empire mahogany furniture (c1815-1840) was handmade, spool furniture was machined. Resembled a string of spools, knobs, or buttons. Usually stained mahogany. Almost a country type. Lathe made straight turnings easier than curved ones so curved bedstead headboards are later and probably date to mid 1800's. | Early bed frames were of hard woods. Mostly maple. Some cherry and walnut. Soft woods later. Pine after 1850. |
| Hitchcock's fancy chairs | 1820-1850 | Mass produced. Stencilled with designs in bright paint. Signed on back edge of seat with some form of Hitchcock name. Shipped knocked down to national market. Other companies made fancy chairs also. | Soft woods. Combination of woods. |
| Gothic | 1820-1850 but mainly 1840's | Light appearing. Tracery, points, arches, like church window. Not a great deal made. Patterned after gothic architecture. | Walnut |

## Mid Victorian 1840-1880

| Name of Style | Dates | Characteristics | Wood |
|---|---|---|---|
| Louis XV | 1840-1865 | French style that imitated Louis XV (reigned 1715-1774). Rococo (rock, shell, flora, fauna) carvings. Elliptical shapes more than round. Curves, not straight lines, advocated. Marble tops. Rich upholstery fabrics but horsehair predominated. Fancy handles of carved wood. Cabriole legs. | Walnut, some rosewood and mahogany. |
| Cottage Furniture | 1845-1890 | Country type, inexpensive. Simple lines. Painted and stencilled with fruits, sheaves of wheat, flowers. Often artificially grained to resemble a more expensive wood. | Pine |
| Renaissance Revival | 1850-1885 | Revival of interest in ancient Greek and Roman culture. Elaborate carving. Heavy, imposing pieces. Much marble. High huge bed frames. Massive, extensively ornamented. | Walnut |

## Late Victorian 1870-1900

| Name of Style | Dates | Characteristics | Wood |
|---|---|---|---|
| Eastlake | 1870-1890 | Rebellion against fancy furniture led by England's Eastlake. Tried to bring design into furniture but simplicity was overwhelmed by machine details. Rectangular lines advocated. | Walnut followed by oak emphasis. Walnut getting scarce. |
| Jacobean | 1870-1880 | Flat, wide decorative moldings. Spindled railings on shelves and table edges. High back, rectangular chairs. | Oak |
| Oriental Influence | 1876-1900 | Lacquer. Fretwork. Chinese-look carving. Bamboo turnings. | Bamboo turnings. |
| Mission Oak | 1895-1910 | Stained dark. Strong, straight, square, heavy lines. Functional furniture. Leather upholstery. | Oak stained dark. |

Brass and iron beds appeared in 1880's.

Golden oak (yellowish varnish) ushered in new century (1900-1915).

---

Perhaps the easiest way to classify the post-Empire American furniture of the 1800's is to call it early, mid, and late Victorian. The spool style will be rated "early" even though it remained around throughout most of the period. Since 1840-1880 represents the time when walnut predominated, these years with Louis XV and the Renaissance Revival styles will be placed in a prominent position. From the late section, Eastlake will receive attention.

Add three objects . . . a child, a box of empty spools, several long shoe laces. The sum equals creative play. A spool necklace, a piled up Leaning Tower of Pisa, a choo-choo train, or a giraffe may appear. Similar imagination helped craftsmen back in the mid-1600's employ decorative ball turnings which became the ancestors of spool furniture, the most common type of turned work in the early and middle 1800's in the United States.

When power driven machines were developed which facilitated creating in wood, spool turnings were found on the earliest products. While ponderous American Empire furniture was constructed mainly from mahogany by hand from about 1810 to 1840, spool furniture was a machine effort from the 1820's to circa 1870, and generally early examples were of hard woods (maple, cherry or walnut). Legs, stretchers, or entire bed frames were made of "spools", and turnings could be sliced down through the middle to become applied decorations on chests or desks. The majority was given a mahogany stain. Using lathes, it was easier to produce rolls of spools, buttons, or knobs in precise lines than those with curves so the earlier bedstead headboards have a straight construction. Generally, by the mid-century, machinists were curving their lines and hard woods had yielded to pine.

In 1850, with gusto and ballyhoo, showman Phineas T. Barnum presented singer Jenny Lind, "The Swedish Nightingale", to American audiences, and so delighted was the populace with her that furniture makers dubbed the currently popular spool bedsteads "Jenny Lind beds" in her honor.

Furniture with such button-type turnings was produced for the common buyer and almost could typify a country style. It reached its zenith in the mid-1800's but is still created today.

Graceful, gentle, curvaceous, flowing— these are words which characterize French Louis the Fifteenth furniture (reigned 1715-1774) which the eclectic machinists of the mid-Victorian era found pleasing. Caressing curves were to be desired while severe angles, straight lines, and the rectangle were shunned. Elliptical shapes predominated over round ones. The cabriole leg with its double curve held allure as it bulged at the knee, recessed in, then swept outward again at the foot to form a line of beauty. Ornamentation was important and designs stressed a rococo feel, a term that comes from the corruption of two French words which mean rock and shell and refers to carvings which receive their inspiration from natural motifs such as flowers, birds, acorns, grapes, other fruits, or leaves. Finger molding was considered attractive.

A leading rococo exponent was the renowned New York cabinetmaker, John Belter (1795-1865). He laminated wood, steamed and bent it, then pierced and seemingly tortured it with carvings to make exotic furniture which now is heralded as museum quality craftsmanship. Rosewood was a favorite with him.

This style merged into the Victorian Renaissance Revival which continued the elaborate nature based carvings. Pieces were ponderous, heavily ornamented, carved with wide scrolled moldings, and yielded an exotic appearance which commanded and demanded attention. (Who could miss eight foot beds and secretaries and sideboards with pretentious carvings, moldings, and veneer work?) Marble received an elite ranking from both Louis XV and Renaissance advocates.

And then along came Charles Lock Eastlake, the non-conformist (1836-1906). As an English architect who was interested in both the outside construction and inner furnishings of the homes he designed, he complained that the furniture of his day was flimsy and minus styling. Rectilinear forms and geometric designs were more pleasing to him than curves which destroyed strength, lacked comfort, and wasted wood; so he wrote a book entitled **Hints on Household Taste, Furnishings, Upholstery and Other Details,** published in 1868, which expanded his thesis.

Unfortunately, machines were new toys and the men who ran them were willing to accept his box outline, but could not resist adding unnecessary embellishments with machined groves, spindles, chip carving, moldings, turnings, brackets and additional appendages which could almost overpower, making a mockery of their mentor's simplicity theme. While much of the English Eastlake was in oak, walnut examples appeared in the United States.

The terminating years of the nineteenth century brought changes in the industry caused by the scarcity of walnut and, because others besides Eastlake complained that utilitarian objects were overly decorated and ponderous, specialists were employed to design furniture. As one of the advertisements stated, draughtsmen were "constantly getting up new designs" to "please the taste of this fast age".

Originally, transportation was a problem. If water routes were followed, they connected specific ports only and were clogged with ice to become impassable during the winter. Roads overland were rutted and rough and wagon wheels could bog down in mud. Plank roads helped to counteract this as logs were sunk into the ground at intervals to provide support for the vehicle wheels. Then, puffing and chugging, trains came along. When products were going to points connected by rail, shipping problems eased. It became possible to charter and load railroad cars with furniture and sell and take orders in the towns along the tracks.

To save space and expense, factories sometimes shipped certain pieces "knocked down" in almost lumber form, and they were assembled by the recipient. If women were unable to work away from home, jobs such as weaving cane chair seats were farmed out to them with the factory responsible for delivering and picking up anywhere in their city. In addition, children were encouraged to participate in such projects. At one time, "traveller's samples", exact replicas of merchandise available, were carried about by salesmen to show tradesmen so they could select what to purchase. The development of photography changed this in 1862 when a salesman from Grand Rapids had furniture photographed. The pictures were made into phamphlets which prospective buyers examined. Thus full scale samples or small models became unnecessary.

In 1861, one Grand Rapids company opened a wareroom in Peoria, Illinois, where furniture could be displayed and sold. This proved so successful that a display area was established in St. Louis also. When Philadelphia's Centennial Exposition in 1876 accorded Grand Rapids world attention for prize winning furniture, the factories there decided to sponsor a local market to put their products on display. That developed into semiannual lavish fairs.

If someone from today's world walked into such an exhibit, a shocked reaction might result. Gould & Co., Philadelphia, in an 1876 ad in **Harper's Weekly** declared that a solid walnut seven piece "parlor suit" in hair cloth or any color wool terry would be shipped any place in the world for sixty-five dollars. Plush or silk upholstery was one hundred and twenty-five dollars. The sofa was medallion backed while the side chairs were the balloon back type. This same company offered a centennial marble "chamber suit" consisting of three pieces created in Renaissance styling for forty seven dollars, including a double bed, bureau, and washstand.

And do you own a somnoe, a meridenne, a toilet, plate, a deck, or a fall leaf? Would it surprise you to hear that currently a somnoe, a bedside table with one drawer and a door, is called a commode? People speak of fainting couches now but the name "meridienne" was a carry over from the French Empire period and originally referred to a short sofa with one arm higher than the other. A "toilet" derives its name from a term for grooming and is a mirror while a plate of glass is a looking glass. Decks are small drawers frequently placed one on either side of Victorian chest tops. Moderns dub them handkerchief boxes, and a fall leaf has now become a drop leaf on a table. Other changes in terminology were noted in Grand Rapids literature of the 1800's so if you find a "secret drawer" in the apron of your chest of drawers, don't expect to discover treasures. It was a slipper drawer where bedroom slippers were stored.

A catalog published when the United States was one hundred years old states: "In submitting our revised 'Wholesale Price List', we desire to say that we always furnish a good article, latest styles and fine finish, and keep on hand a very extensive stock, by which we are enabled to fill orders promptly.

"Terms

. . . We will not be responsible for releases, or overcharges by railroads, nor for breakage or damage, after leaving our Warerooms . . .Charges for packing reasonable and done by experienced hands.

"Explanations

The width given in Bedsteads is the width between Side Rails, or length of Bed Slats. The height given of Bedsteads is the highest part of Head Boards.

Twelve cents reduction made on Bedsteads without Slats.

We ship What-Nots, Cribs, Stands and Towel Racks 'knock down,' unless otherwise ordered.

Burlap or Mats used in packing taken back at amount charged, when returned within thirty days—after goods are shipped—and charges prepaid . . .

NELSON, MATTER & CO.

Grand Rapids, March 1st, 1876."

The Madison, Indiana, newspaper **The Spirit of the Age,** June 29, 1874, announces that a furniture retailer has "all varieties of CASES and COFFINS", and other ads indicate furniture factories included these articles in their production. They took care of their customers' needs very extensively because a person could be conceived in one of their beds and, at death, could be concealed in one of their coffins.

It is interesting that the machine age brought a middle class to the fore who could afford to buy comfortable attractive furnishings for their homes. The country was expanding and so was the population; thus, there were more houses being built to provide a market for mass made items. No longer did a customer confer with a cabinet-maker to dictate what carvings to include or to suggest structural changes in furniture. Shops kept stock designs on hand readily available to a wide range of customers at a lower price than formerly because factories could turn out articles more rapidly than home craftsmen could. Thus, not only was the nineteenth century characterized by the entrance of mass production, but also it was distinct because purchasing power was opened extensively to the masses and no longer was restricted mainly to the affleunt.

# Chapter 3
## The Dramatic Entrance

A hall's function may be trite, merely a way to get from one room to another, or it may be enticing. At "Wheatland" where America's only Bachelor President, James Buchanan (1791-1868) lived, it was the latter. A row of elaborate imported crystal candle chandeliers are accommodated easily by the twelve foot ceilings. The President was a tall man for his times, over six feet, and even he did not need to fear hitting the many dangling, sparkling prisms. Two oval brass girandoles with mirrors flank either side of the doorway in the hall. Placed too high to serve as looking glasses, their purpose was to reflect the light of the candles, not images, and provide illumination, not promote vanity. When lighted, the candles reflect in all the glass and produce a glittering avenue of radiance. Now, that's a dramatic entrance which invites guests in and makes them eager to see the rest of the mansion.

While most hallways were not so generous in proportions and so expensive in decor, most offered somewhere for a guest and family members to deposit outer garments when they came in.

Functioning almost as a butler, a free-standing hall stand occupied the entrance area of homes to receive hats, coats, and dripping umbrellas. Usually this article of furniture incorporated a mirror so that milady could adjust her hair on arrival and her hat at departure time. Dapper gentlemen could be served in a similar manner. The size, shape, and the material from which it was constructed varied, and the mirror could be small, medium, or floor length.

Stationary or adjustable, fancy or plain brass or iron hooks or wooden knobs, sometimes with porcelain tips, held the discarded outer appeal while an arm permitted closed umbrellas to stand erect as water slithered off into drip pans at the base. Those removable-for-dumping, small metal containers could be fancy, taking on a shell shape for example, or simple and might be cast from pot metal or brass. Some styles of hall stands incorporated a drawer, a marble slab, or a wooden shelf. Pieces of this nature may be referred to as umbrella stands, although most commonly this functional furnishing is called a hall tree by moderns.

Hat racks were utilized too. One common Victorian hat rack which hung on the wall has become known as an accordian type because when it is collapsed together, it resembles a squeezed tight accordian. Many were made of walnut, their screwed in wooden pegs tipped with porcelain. As the name indicates, hats could be suspended on the pegs. Another type was a utilitarian variety which was also attached to the wall but had a straight board background and a row of metal hooks. There were also wall ones with rectangular lines which included a mirror. Wheel shapes could be long or short. These were essential items because closets were not incorporated in most houses in those days.

Pier mirrors might be found in some portion of a hallway. These ranged from a size which hung over a table or chest to a floor-length standing type. Some varieties, also called petticoat mirrors, were under a table so that women could flounce past and glance in to be sure that their floor sweeping skirts were adjusted properly. Ordinarily a long pier mirror was scaled to occupy a place between two tall floor-to-ceiling windows or some other narrow space. A marble or wooden shelf could be included.

These were functional furnishings such as would be utilized in most Victorian homes.

HALL TREE—6' 11", fret top, pierced back, applied ornaments, marble top shelf over drawer.

$550.00 - 600.00

HALL TREE—7' 4", molded and incised pediment, burl veneer raised panels, pierced back, marble shelf over drawer. $750.00 - 800.00

HALL TREE—7' 4", molded and paneled pediment, burl veneer raised panels, pierced back, applied ornaments, etching on mirror, marble shelf over drawer.

$625.00 - 725.00

HALL TREE—7' 3", pierced and carved pediment, recessed and raised burl veneer panels, applied molding, metal hat hooks, marble shelf over drawer. (Eastlake style) $700.00 - 750.00

HALL TREE—7′ 7″, molded and carved pediment, pierced raised panels, circular molding, applied ornaments, finials, wooden top over drawer. **$700.00 - 750.00**

HALL TREE—8′ 1″, carved pediment, burl veneer raised panels, applied ornaments, finials, marble top over drawer. **$900.00 - 1,000.00**

HALL TREE—7′ 7″, carved and molded pediment, pierced raised panels, applied ornaments, finials, marble top over drawer.

$575.00 - 675.00

HAT RACK—32″ x 32″, molded frame, ring molding around mirror.

$200.00 - 250.00

HAT RACK—25″ x 28″, incised lines, porcelain tipped, converted to bric a brac shelf.

$55.00 - 75.00

PIER MIRROR—7′ 6″, burl veneer raised panels, applied ornaments, lift lid box at base. (pediment not original)

**$500.00 - 600.00**

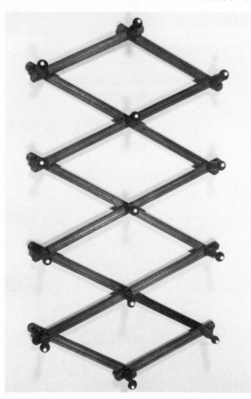

HAT RACK—19″ x 36″, incised lines, porcelain tipped, accordian type.

$55.00 - 75.00

PIER MIRROR—7′ 1″, burl veneer raised panels, applied ornaments, urn finials on molded pediment, marble top over drawer.

**$550.00 - 650.00**

PIER MIRROR—7′ 10″, machine lines and carving, pilasters, molded and incised pediment, marble top over drawer. (Eastlake style)

**$600.00 - 650.00**

PIER MIRROR—8′ 10″, burl veneer raised panels, applied ornaments, molded and paneled pediment, serpentine marble top over base.

**$750.00 - 850.00**

# Chapter 4
## Step Into My Parlor

Many Victorian homes were designed with a sitting room which served just that purpose and a parlor which could remain shut off from the rest of the house. This latter was a special room with the best furniture kept clean and fancy for social events such as when the parson, favorite relatives, or daughter's best beau came to call. Here also, the coffin might be placed when a family member "passed on". Furniture in these rooms could vary, and many people now think that the nineteenth century was characterized by stiff, formal, uncomfortable seating.

Sofas, love seats, and settees are elongated chairs made to accommodate more than one person and usually they follow the current chair designs. The term "sopha" is Arabic in origin. Pretend you are plodding over desert sands on the rocking broad back of a camel, your only relief a cushion ("sopha") on the animal's saddle. It does not suggest comfort. Yet, in about 1680, the French borrowed this name to apply to a long upholstered seat for two or more. This appears to be the first mention of such an article of furniture with its attached back and upholstered seat and arms. In the 1700's, the French originated upholstered pieces with coil springs. Prior to that a stuffing of such things as feathers, wool or hair was placed over a webbed frame to provide a soft, comfortable seat. Although sofas became part of the home furnishings in England around the second decade of the eighteenth century, the earliest examples in this country were probably made in Philadelphia around 1826, a little over one hundred years later.

A love seat (or "courting chair") is generally considered seating for two and because of its connotation as a cozy spot for couples only, it acquired that name. At first a love seat resembled a pair of chairs joined together with the middle set of legs and arms missing so as to form one unit.

A settee can be about twice the width of a chair or longer. It may be upholstered, especially on the seat, and may retain exposed wood on the back. Usually a sofa features both an upholstered back and seat and rates higher in the comfort category than does a settee. It is also made to accommodate several sitters.

Frames varied. There were gentle appearing ones with finger roll outlines and at the other extreme ones which gave the feeling that the wood was tortured with much piercing and bending. An oval or rounded wooden loop in the middle of a sofa back which frames some of the fabric may be designated a cameo, medallion, or mirror back by today's terminology. When the frame writhes about, its lines resemble those of a snake wiggling, and it is referred to as "serpentine" in structure. High points (of which there may be as many as three with the central one commonly the peak) are called "crestings". Some of these wooden crestings have pegs on them and may be removed from the frame. Roses were a favorite decoration but carvings such as nuts, grapes, and leaves prevailed also.

Plain velvet, plush, satin, brocatel, and damask were available for upholstering, but somber black horsehair was almost a trademark of the times. Haircloth was woven from strands extracted from the mane and tail of horses combined with linen threads, and children too tiny to touch the floor in a normal flat-footed fashion found its surface so slippery that they had to brace their toes on the floor and push back in order to keep from slipping off the seats. If they could sneak into the parlor unsupervised, they could slide gleefully off the sofa making a game of its slippery qualities. Often buttons were sewn through the upholstery fabric and stuffing to hold the filling in place. The arrangement of the buttons and the resulting folds in the material formed patterns, and this is referred to as tufting or button tufting.

For today's long legged people, furniture from the past century may be too small for comfort since the pieces often have narrow seats and are built close to the floor. In the nursery tale about the "Three Bears", Papa had a huge chair, Mama a medium size, and Baby a small one. Parlor suites seemed to incorporate this idea since there are rare French inspired frames that appear to be almost for Baby Bear in spite of the fact that they are adult editions. Other sets may retain the fragile look when they are larger in structure, but few seem to encourage reclining.

While currently, interior designers feel that a room has more vitality if it displays a variety of furnishings which are compatible but not all of the exact same style and time period, look alikes were preferred by Victorian home owners. A "parlor suit" could consist of from three to seven pieces. The larger suit had a sofa or love seat, four side chairs, a version with partial arms, and a larger chair which, while straight, gave some promise of ease with its padded arms. The carvings, leg style, turnings, and upholstery fabric in all seven articles matched precisely.

Price variations occurred according to such factors as the number of pieces, the ornateness of the carving and veneer, the workmanship, and the upholstery fabric selected. In the 1860's, one manufacturer offered a five piece "stuffed back" parlor suit for twenty four dollars while a competitor turned out a sofa with six chairs for the same price.

Mitchell & Rammelsberg Furniture Co., in an ad in the **Indianapolis Daily Sentinel,** April 16, 1874, invited readers to "See our parlor suits for $50 & a $1000".

An 1873 seven piece set created from black walnut with damask upholstery cost the John Monzel firm of Chicago one thousand dollars to manufacture.

Names can change through the years, and the lounging or arm chair of the 1800's currently is called a gentleman's or Mr. chair while its counterpart is known as a lady's or Mrs. version. Now one hears the short arms of the latter termed demi-arms or hip rests, and such a chair was slightly wider and more gracious than the small side chairs. Then, as now, homemakers spent hours preparing needlepoint coverings to enhance chair seats and backs. Utilitarian white porcelain casters were considered modish and conformed to the lines of the furniture to which they were attached instead of being stuck on sort of as an after thought.

An odd place to sit was provided by a corner chair. It almost had a maladjusted appearance because the seat was constructed in a diamond shape with one of its legs (a fancy one) at the center front point. This was a novelty, but a type which was developed greatly during the 1800's was the rocker. Many authorities feel that chairs with runners on them were an American invention prior to the mid-1700's, and some like to credit creative Benjamin Franklin of lightning rod, stove, and bifocal glasses fame with their appearance. Others say an unremembered someone took the rockers off a cradle and joined them to a straight chair with its legs cut shorter to form the first rocking chair.

At any rate, Ben ordered some "crook't feet" chairs as the 1740's terminated. One early name for the narrow runners was "carpet cutters" since they could be hard on floor coverings. The rockers were inserted into niches in the legs and doweled or pinned in place. European travelers who visited this country made fun of this rustic American innovation and were afraid they might tilt over backwards if they sat in such creeping contraptions. At first the runners extended about equidistant in front and back, but it was found that greater stability developed if the curved slats protruded further to rearward. Another discovery was that broader rockers helped establish a firmer base, and by 1854, such a chair could bear a five dollar price tag.

Victorians appeared to enjoy rocking, and it seems as if almost every conceivable type of chair was placed on runners to provide comfort. There were all wooden varieties plus cane seat styles or those with both woven seats and backs. These could have round or rectangular contours or combine both lines, and arms came square, rounded, as demi-arms, or might be lacking altogether. Folding fireside rockers were small, easily portable, and often employed a carpet type upholstery material to become "carpet rockers". When a seat was not very high off the floor, it might have been used when a man was removing his boots or a lady her shoes to replace them with slippers. This gave the wearer a place to sit in comfort so he or she did not have to bend or stoop. Therefore, the name "slipper rocker" was applied to a low chair, and there were examples without rockers called slipper chairs.

Rockers could have upholstered seats, but there were also gracious versions with carved ornamentation or finger roll frames which resembled gentlemen or ladies' chairs with runners incorporated. The proprietor of Ford Theater in Washington, D.C. knew that President Lincoln liked a rocking chair, and so he placed one in the Presidential box. The Chief Executive was sitting in it that fatal night when an assassin fired his destructive shot. Honest Abe owned a favorite one with a padded seat and back and rounded wooden arms. Since there is a tendency to name articles after famous people, similar chairs have become known as Lincoln rockers.

By the end of the 1800's, patented types employed platforms and springs. On these the rectangular lines the English architect Charles Eastlake advocated predominated.

Desks were common sitting room case pieces. Sometimes one wonders. How could a box go through the process of evolution and come out a desk? It happened. Prior to the late 1600's, such an item of furniture was not in use. Rather, portable Bible and writing boxes, small enough to be lifted easily, were made. When someone decided to place a stand-like frame beneath these boxes, the desk idea was beginning to germinate.

Bible boxes did not have provisions for a lock because not even a fiend would dare to steal the Holy Book. But, a desk was different. Important papers and letters were kept within so locks were essential, plus camouflaged columns which pulled out to house documents, and hidey holes and secret drawers where treasures could be stuffed, in a time period which predated the use of banks or safety deposit vaults.

Creative cabinet makers of the late 1600's and early 1700's must have enjoyed varying and changing the box until they came up with a desk which allowed a person knee room for comfortable sitting, adequate storage space, and a sufficient writing surface. Someone added a sloping lid with hinges at the top. When the lid was raised, backwards away from the user, a storage space was exposed. Closed, there was a place for writing or for propping a book while reading. Early school desks often followed this general idea; however, each time a student desired something stored inside, the top had to be cleared and raised in order to secure the needed item.

This arrangement was inconvenient and another idea was tried. The hinges were placed at the bottom so that the slanting front, when open, dropped down. Often two recessed slides, one on either side, pulled out to provide support. Sometimes chains caught and held the lid in place. The dropped top offered a convenient writing area, and the owner had ample leg space underneath. The pigeon holes and drawers inside the recessed space were now more readily accessible. Gradually the empty frame was replaced by a series of drawers so that the user had an added attraction— adequate space for filing various supplies. Another craftsman decided to place book shelves above the desk. This type, with a chest of three or four drawers beneath, a slanting drop lid for writing and a glass enclosed cupboard above, became known as a secretary. As a deviation, a cylinder constructed from a solid piece of wood and fashioned in a quarter round hood shape rolled forward to provide a cover for the pigeon hole storage unit and the writing surface. Examples are called cylinder desks, and some include a bookcase section while others don't. Secretary desks can be constructed as one unit while in others the top and base can be separated.

Through the year various names have been developed for corresponding pieces of furniture. Some desks resemble a table, with a drawer in it for the base, and an upper cupboard storage unit with pigeon holes and small drawers. The covering lid, often held by chains, drops down to form a writing surface. Many authorities call this a student desk while common folk, taking the name of a famous gentleman of the period, select the descriptive title "Lincoln desk". The unimaginative description in a Grand Rapids 1876 list is "fall leaf desk with table". Quite often a square type leg with a few turnings was utilized, and these are at times called "New York legs". There may be a compartment at the top with a lid that raises up. So called "plantation desks" were similar but had a two door cabinet above the table base with its fall leaf. Some required a long legged stool as the accompanying seat. An overseer's desk had a slant top, tall legs and also required a stool or a standing worker. These names may be local in derivation.

Parlor desks were inclined to be small and dainty. Frequently a desk front pulls down to form a flat writing surface and behind it is housed various sized pigeon holes, or there may be a rolltop. The base contains a full length drawer and a door which opens to shelves inside. There are also desk tops which rest upon what appears to be a three drawer chest base. Sometimes the desk is one piece, sometimes two. Currently these are called "lady's desks", but in an 1873 catalog, the name is "parlor desk".

To most people, a davenport suggests a comfortable place to sit, but to an antiquer, it can conjure up a picture of a small desk with a unique feature. The drawers do not face the user. Instead, they open out at the side, and there may be similar blind drawers opposite to provide balance. The slant top (called book slide in early catalogs) has an overhang under which the user's knees go. Hinged at the rear, the top lifts so a storage compartment can be reached. In an 1870's catalog this style is listed as a lady's desk, and there is no mention of a "davenport".

"This desk is meant for standing" might be a line to describe a bureau desk. It resembled a tall chest of drawers but one of the top drawers is a fake with a false front which drops open to form a short writing surface with compact storage compartments to the rear. Retractable wooden slides, one on either side, could hold the drop portion or it could be supported by brackets or a chain. A bookcase top may be included.

A table desk with two side by side drawers was considered an office table, while a version which is currently referred to as a Wells Fargo has an 1873 catalog title of "business desk, hinged cornice". Its two doors open on pigeon holes and the top apron lifts to display added filing space while the writing surface is provided by a table with a top which slants toward the user.

As might be expected, Renaissance lines were highly decorated. An Eastlake type desk might have a drop front or a cylinder arrangement which closed off the pigeon holes and small inner drawers. A railing with carved medallions might frame the top.

Tables are also necessary equipment in a sitting room or parlor. Parlor tables (listed as center tables in a factory price book) popular in the mid-1800's were frequently oval in shape with wooden or marble tops. Some ornate ones are now known as turtle tops even though they may have been called serpentine when originally made. "Scalloped" was another catalog name for tops cut in irregular curves. During the Renaissance influence, patches of decorative veneer, carvings, applied circles, and hanging finials added additional fussiness. Urns set in the base amid a maze of curving legs were considered elite, and a carved animal might provide added elegance. Rectangular tables were prominent at the end of the century.

Small round tables with pedestal bases (called "pillar" in literature from the late 1800's) functioned as Bible, plant, lamp, or candle stands. These might have marble tops either recessed or raised. Large round tables were prevalent, and the aprons frequently were enhanced with carvings or fancy veneers. When open carving was used, it was referred to as fretwork, and crestings displayed it to advantage.

Sofa tables were usually ovals with marble tops and yellow (or Sienna) marble was considered especially attractive, costing twice as much originally as a white surface. There should be a well frame beneath the marble to hold it, and if there is a wooden top underneath, one may be suspicious that the marble is a later addition.

There was a special gaming table also. Residents of the more liberal British colonies in America (never Puritanical New England) enjoyed playing cards for money in the mid-1700's. Craftsmen created a table for this purpose that at first was known as a "loo" table since the game played was "loo". Early examples had four oval cut-in pockets, one to the left of each player. These were guinea pockets after an early English gold coin of that name. They held the forfeit money. Places designed for candles were found at each corner so the table would be well lit.

Such tables were functional because most could be folded to form smaller units when they were not needed for game playing purposes. Some could be placed in three positions. On a square one, the top was hinged in half to fold down double thus forming a small rectangle. Folded round versions condensed to a semi-circle. At times the top leaf was constructed to flip up to stand against the wall. Others were fall leaf in construction. Occasionally a fifth leg might swing out to catch the leaf so the double rectangle would form a square or the half circle would become complete and large enough to accommodate four chairs for a session of cards. Tables could be fashioned with a pillar (pedestal) base or a quartet of legs and the top could pivot to expose a compartment underneath in the apron for storing games. When the top was swiveled ninety degrees to the correct position, a firm playing surface resulted. Round versions of these multi-position tables were not quite so common. Names applied are game, gaming, deal, or card table.

There was another tricky table. Tilt top (or tip-up or tip top) tables were known as far back as medieval times; however, it was eighteenth century craftsmen who developed them to their finest. During the Queen Anne period (c 1690-1710) expensive precious tea was imported from the Orient and the English established a daily ritual of drinking this exotic new beverage. Naturally, special tables were devised to hold the tea service, and the tilt top was one of the popular types employed. Victorian homemakers of the next century liked them too, and so factories continued to produce them.

Although usually round, they could be octagonal. The top was hinged to the pillar base (pedestal) in such a manner that it tipped to a vertical position as a space saver when not needed. The surface might be decorated with inlay, and this showed off well when the top was positioned in a perpendicular manner. Scrolled or piecrust edges sometimes occurred and resembled the way housewives crimp crusts on pies they bake.

Functional worktables made their appearance in the 1600's. A common form for seamstresses in the 1700's and early 1800's had two drawers with a cloth bag hanging down underneath to hold sewing necessities. It could be called a bag, work, or sewing table. Styles changed to meet specific needs, to express the creative urge of the craftsman, or to fulfill the desires of clients. Worktables for writing or sewing might have hinged tops which lifted up or drawers which contained compartments for a variety of sewing accessories or paper supplies. A sewing stand with a shelf and one with a drawer were two varieties Nelson, Matter & Co. of Grand Rapids made in the 1870's. There were also versions for games, reading, dressing, drawing or tea serving which did not vary too much in appearance from the other small utilitarian forms. Some were bedroom pieces while others fit into the sitting room or parlor decor.

Yet another type of furnishing could be utilized in various rooms. Clutter seems characteristic of Victorian tastes, and ladies in the nineteenth century arranged their glass trinkets, elaborately bound books, souvenir items, statuettes, pottery, or other treasures on whatnots which revealed this bric-a-brac handsomely. Impressed by French names, the fashionable referred to these display stands as "etagères", a name derived from "etage" meaning a story or division to indicate the series of shelves which composed the unit. Some incorporated a central drawer or a slab of marble and such stands were equally at ease in the parlor, sitting room, library, or nursery.

Today the name "etagère" seems to be reserved for a towering fancy kind with a vast carved walnut frame and a large mirror surrounded by shelves for treasures. It is an impressive, tall piece of furniture. The more common version with four or five graduating shelves stood in a corner or against a wall. Hanging types were available and much less expensive. The backs of the shelves often featured fret, a border with an ornamental design.

One sitting room or bedroom accessory is small but significant. Stretching ones feet out from a comfortable chair and onto a footstool suggest relaxing comfort. A walnut frame, with stuffing covered with upholstery materials current for the period including needle work done by the women, made them attractive. Shapes varied with oval and round versions as well as scrolls and rectangles available.

Footrests could be squat or stand fairly tall, and one with a dual purpose was handy in the bedroom. It had a lift top so that slippers could be stored in it. Appropriately, it was known as a "footrest with slipper box" and was usually a taller, slim rectangular shape with a padded cover. The walnut bases could have intricate patterns.

Another accessory item was the magazine rack which stood near a chair so that anyone sitting there could reach down to find reading material. **Godey's Magazine and Lady's Book, Harper's, The Art Amateur,** a **Monthly Journal Devoted to the Cultivation of Art in the Household,** or religious publications might be held erect in this frame which could be ornate or plain.

The retreat for the male who dominated the Victorian household was the library lined with his choice of books. He censored the reading material and eliminated frivolous novels which did not promote good morals, educate, or prove satisfying culturally. Naturally, bookcases were necessary to hold the many leather bound volumes.

Tall ones with glass doors and with a drawer or two at the base were commonly made in walnut. Library tables could have a shelf base where periodicals could be stacked. Others had a stretcher type construction.

With all these furnishings available, is it any wonder that Victorians were accused of enjoying clutter?

SIDE CHAIR—oval back, finger roll, carved cresting. (Louis XV substyle)

**$200.00 - 225.00**

SIDE CHAIR—applied burl veneer panels, carved and molded cresting, demi-arms. (Renaissance-Eastlake influence)

**$125.00 - 150.00**

SIDE CHAIR—applied burl veneer panels, applied ornaments, molded cresting, demi-arms. (Louis XVI influence)
$150.00 - 175.00

SIDE CHAIR—burl veneer banding and applied panels, machine lines and carving, demi-arms. (Eastlake)
$125.00 - 150.00

SIDE CHAIR—machine lines and carving, molded crest, demi-arms. (Eastlake)

$125.00 - 150.00

SIDE CHAIR—machine lines, demi-arms. (Eastlake)
$75.00 - 100.00

SIDE CHAIR—machine lines and carving, demi-arms. (Eastlake)

$100.00 - 125.00

SIDE CHAIR—machine lines and carving, applied burl veneer panels, demi-arms. (Eastlake)

$100.00 - 125.00

SIDE CHAIR—photographer's studio chair or hall chair, applied ornaments, elaborately carved and pierced cresting, supported by turned columns. (Gothic and Renaissance substyles)

$400.00 - 500.00

SIDE CHAIR—low seat 15½″ high, single back piece heavily molded and pierced supported by turned columns, finial ornaments, possible hall location. (Gothic substyle)

$250.00 - 300.00

CORNER CHAIR—burl veneer banding, machine lines and carving. (Eastlake)

$200.00 - 250.00

LADY'S CHAIR—spoon back, simple carved crest. (Louis XV substyle)

$300.00 - 350.00

LADY'S CHAIR—oval finger roll back, simple carved crest. (Louis XV substyle)

$325.00 - 350.00

LADY'S CHAIR—balloon back, finger roll, carved floral crest. (Louis XV substyle)

$350.00 - 375.00

LADY'S CHAIR—oval back, finger roll. (Louis XV substyle)

$325.00 - 375.00

GENTLEMAN'S CHAIR—oval back, finger roll, open arms. (Louis XV substyle)

$300.00 - 350.00

GENTLEMAN'S CHAIR—finger roll, applied burl veneer panel near curved crest, button tufting. (Louis XV substyle)

$325.00 - 375.00

GENTLEMAN'S CHAIR—oval back, finger roll, open arms, button tufting. (Louis XV substyle)

$325.00 - 375.00

GENTLEMAN'S CHAIR—oval back, finger roll, open arms, button tufting. (Louis XV substyle)
$300.00 - 350.00

ARM CHAIR—machine lines and carving, burl banding near crest, open arms. (Eastlake)
$125.00 - 175.00

ARM CHAIR—incised lines, open arms, button tufting. (Louis XVI with Eastlake influence)
$150.00 - 175.00

ARM CHAIR—machine lines and carving, open arms. (Eastlake)
$125.00 - 175.00

ARM CHAIR—machine lines and carving, open arms. (Eastlake)

$125.00 - 175.00

ARM CHAIR—curved wooden frame, open arms, platform type base.

$125.00 - 150.00

MATCHING LADY'S AND GENTLEMAN'S CHAIRS—
oval backs, finger roll, open arms, button tufting. (Louis XV substyle)

$750.00 - 850.00 set

**MATCHING LADY'S AND GENTLEMAN'S CHAIRS—**
oval backs, finger roll, open arms, burl veneer panel in
molded crests. (Louis XV substyle) **$750.00 - 800.00 set**

**MATCHING LADY'S AND GENTLEMAN'S CHAIRS—**
balloon backs, carved crests, finger roll, button tufting;
matching scroll footstools. (Louis XV substyle)
**$850.00 - 1,000.00 set**

**FOLDING FIRE SIDE CHAIR**

$150.00 - 175.00

ROCKING CHAIR—oval caned back with demi-arms, round caned seat.

$175.00 - 225.00

ROCKING CHAIR—oval caned back with arms, U shaped caned seat.

$200.00 - 250.00

ROCKING CHAIR—caned back surmounted by machine carved turnings and incised crest rail, square caned seat, demi-arms. (Eastlake)

$150.00 - 175.00

ROCKING CHAIR—rectangular caned back, applied burl veneer panels on crest rail, round caned seat, demi-arms.
**$150.00 - 175.00**

ROCKING CHAIR—rectangular caned back, arms and back in a continuous curve, burl veneer band near crest, U shaped caned seat.
**$175.00 - 200.00**

ROCKING CHAIR—rectangular caned back, roll arms, U shaped caned seat. (Lincoln type)
**$200.00 - 250.00**

ROCKING CHAIR—rectangular caned back with arms, burl veneer bands near crest, machine lines, square caned seat. (Eastlake)
**$175.00 - 225.00**

ROCKING CHAIR—rectangular caned back, roll arms, U shaped caned seat, serpentine front, concave front rung. (Lincoln type)  **$200.00 - 225.00**

ROCKING CHAIR—upholstered, open arms, floral carved crest.  **$225.00 - 275.00**

ROCKING CHAIR—spindle, spool back with arms, upholstered seat.  **$150.00 - 175.00**

ROCKING CHAIR—upholstered, open arms, floral carved crest, applied burl veneer panels.  **$225.00 - 275.00**

ROCKING CHAIR—upholstered, simple flowing wooden frame.

$175.00 - 200.00

ROCKING CHAIR—upholstered, balloon back, finger roll, carved floral crest. (Louis XV substyle)

$200.00 - 250.00

ROCKING CHAIR—upholstered, closed arms, balloon back, finger roll. (Louis XV substyle)

$275.00 - 325.00

ROCKING CHAIR—upholstered, one piece molded seat and arms.

$200.00 - 225.00

**FOLDING FIRE SIDE ROCKER**
$150.00 - 175.00

**FOLDING FIRE SIDE ROCKER WITH ARMS**
$150.00 - 175.00

**PLATFORM ROCKER**—upholstered, applied burl veneer panels, molded panel on base, molded crest. (Renaissance influence)
$250.00 - 275.00

**PLATFORM ROCKER**—upholstered, applied burl veneer panels, molded panel on base, molded crest. (Renaissance influence)
$225.00 - 250.00

42

PLATFORM ROCKER—upholstered, burl veneer banding, applied ornaments, molded panel on base. (Renaissance influence)                    $225.00 - 250.00

PLATFORM ROCKER—upholstered, machine lines and carving. (Eastlake)

$150.00 - 200.00

PLATFORM ROCKER—upholstered, machine lines and carving. (Eastlake)

$150.00 - 200.00

PLATFORM ROCKER—upholstered, button tufting, applied burl veneer panels, machine lines and carving. (Eastlake)

$175.00 - 200.00

CYLINDER FRONT SECRETARY—6' 10" tall, 38" wide, burl veneer raised panels on drawers, veneered cylinder panels.           **$1,500.00 - 1,750.00**

CYLINDER FRONT SECRETARY—7'3" tall, 41" wide, machine lines and carving, veneered cylinder panels, molded and paneled cornice.     **$1,300.00 - 1,500.00**

CYLINDER FRONT SECRETARY—7' 2" tall, 43" wide, burl veneer raised panels on drawers and bookcase, veneered cylinder panels, applied ornaments.

**$1,600.00 - 1,850.00**

CYLINDER FRONT SECRETARY—8' tall, 44" wide, burl veneer raised panels on drawers and bookcase, veneered cylinder panels, pilasters on lower corner stiles, turned columns, molded and paneled cornice.

**$2,000.00 - 2,250.00**

**CYLINDER FRONT SECRETARY**—7' 1" tall, 38" wide, veneered bands on drawers, veneered cylinder panel, machine lines. **$1,400.00 - 1,600.00**

**CYLINDER FRONT DESK**—5' tall, 31" wide, veneered cylinder panel, machine lines and carving, machine carved and spindled gallery. **$1100.00 - 1200.00**

**CYLINDER FRONT DESK**—4' tall, 32" wide, veneered cylinder panel, applied molding on gallery. **$700.00 - 800.00**

**\*SLANT FRONT SECRETARY**—7' 10" tall, 55" wide, plain front, applied molding on stiles. **$1800.00 - 2000.00**

\*(1876 PRICES—heights to 8' 7" — $37.00 - 55.00)

*SLANT FRONT TABLE SECRETARY—7' 1" tall, 36" wide, raised panels on slant front and drawer, machine lines and carving.          **$1,000.00 - 1,200.00**

*SLANT FRONT SECRETARY—7' tall, 40" wide, molding bands framing slant front and drawer, applied carved ornaments.          **$1000.00 - 1200.00**

*SLANT FRONT SECRETARY—8' tall, 45" wide, burl veneer raised panels on slant front, drawer, and doors, applied molding ornaments on lower stiles.          **$1,400.00 - 1,500.00**

*SLANT FRONT SECRETARY—6' 8½" tall, 39" wide, burl veneer raised panels on molded drawers and bookcase.          **$1,200.00 - 1,400.00**

*(1876 PRICES—heights to 8' 7" — $37.00 - 55.00)

46

**\*SLANT FRONT SECRETARY—7′ 6″ tall, 42″ wide,** circular and beaded molding, chamfered stiles with applied ornaments.                $1400.00 - 1500.00

**PLANTATION DESK—7′ 3″ tall, 36″ wide, lift top lid,** beaded molding, paneled glass.

$900.00 - 1100.00

**SECRETARY WITH FOLD OUT WRITING SURFACE—** 7′ 8″ tall, 45″ wide, circular molding on drawers, fretwork surmounting paneled glass.

$1400.00 - 1500.00

**—DROP FRONT TABLE DESK—4′ 9″ tall, 37¼″ wide,** beaded molding, lift top cornice.        $475.00 - 500.00

\*(1876 PRICES—heights to 8′ 7″ — $37.00 - 55.00)
—(1876 PRICE—$12.00)

—DROP FRONT TABLE DESK—5′ 2″ tall, 36″ wide, machine lines and carving on drop front and gallery.
$425.00 - 500.00

*SLANT FRONT PARLOR DESK—4′ 8″ tall, 30″ wide, burl veneer raised panels, gallery with book shelf supported by turned columns, panel banding, molded pediment.
$650.00 - 800.00

*DROP FRONT PARLOR DESK—4′ 8″ tall, 26″ wide, heavy machine lines and carving, applied ornaments, burl veneer raised panels, veneered upper and lower drawer fronts. (Eastlake)
$850.00 - 900.00

DROP FRONT PARLOR DESK—with trestle base, 4′ tall, 29¼″ wide, burl veneer raised panels
$400.00 - 500.00

—(1876 PRICE—$12.00)
*(1876 PRICE—$43.00)

**SLOPING LIFT LID PARLOR DESK**—with trestle base 3′ 9″ tall, 24″ wide, high gallery with open work, applied pilasters, finials.

$450.00 - 500.00

**BUREAU DESK**—fall front secretary drawer, chamfered stiles with applied spool turnings.

$750.00 - 850.00

**WHATNOT DESK**—fold out writing surface: 5′ 8″ tall, 33″ wide, circular and square applied molding on drawers.

**$650.00 - 750.00**

\*DAVENPORT DESK—sloping lift top, 2′ 6″ tall to front lid, 24″ wide, incised carved gallery, molding bands framing panels and drawers, reeded columns.

**$650.00 - 700.00**

*(1876 PRICES—called Lady's parlor desk — $20.00 - 23.00)

49

BUREAU SECRETARY—6' 9" tall, 44" wide, fall front secretary drawer, chamfered stiles, veneered case, beaded molding.   **$1,400.00 - 1,600.00**

LIFT TOP DESK—35" to front top, 42" wide, top measures 29½" x 42", oversea's type.

**$375.00 - 475.00**

BUREAU SECRETARY—8' 10" tall, 48" wide, fall front secretary drawer, applied ornaments, veneered doors, burl veneer raised panels, molded and paneled pediment.   **$2000.00 - 2200.00**

*OFFICE TABLE DESK—29" x 47", molding bands framing drawers.   **$300.00 - 375.00**

*(1876 PRICES—width 46" to 58" — $10.00 - 13.00)

**SLANT FRONT DESK**—3′ 6″ tall, 42″ wide, pull out slide supports, applied ornaments on corner stiles.

**$550.00 - 600.00**

*BUSINESS DESK**—5′ 2″ tall, 54″ wide, molding bands framing drawers and doors, lift top cornice.

**$950.00 - 1,100.00**

**SLANT FRONT DESK**—4′ 2″ tall, 38½″ wide, pull out slide supports, beaded bands framing drop front and doors, lift top cornice.

**$400.00 - 450.00**

—**CORNER WHATNOT**—4′ 8″ tall, 27″ wide at base, 5 graduated shelves.

**$225.00 - 275.00**

*(1876 PRICE—$32.00)
—(1876 PRICES — $3.00 - 7.50)

51

—CORNER WHATNOT—5′ tall, 25″ wide at base, 5 graduated shelves with fretted backs. **$200.00 - 250.00**

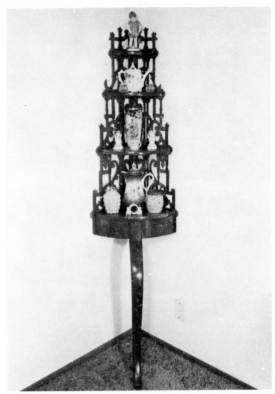

CORNER WHATNOT—6′ tall, single supporting leg, 3 graduated shelves with fretted back. **$400.00 - 425.00**

CORNER WHATNOT—on cupboard base, 4′ 10″ tall, 33″ wide at base, 3 graduated shelves with fretted backs, burl veneer door panel with molding bands, applied arch molding. **$500.00 - 600.00**

*SIDE WHATNOT—4′ 9″ tall, 29″ wide at base, 5 graduated shelves, veneered drawer fronts, fretted sides. **$400.00 - 500.00**

—(1876 PRICES — $3.00 - 750)
*(1876 PRICES — $3.00 - 750)

52

*SIDE WHATNOT—5' 2" tall, 34" wide at base, 5 graduated shelves.
**$275.00 - 300.00**

HANGING WHATNOT—2' 2" tall, 24½" wide, machine lines and applied ornaments.
**$175.00 - 200.00**

*SIDE WHATNOT—5' tall, 36" at base, 5 graduated shelves.
**$250.00 - 300.00**

*(1876 PRICES — $3.00 - 750)

ETAGÈRE WHATNOT—7' 6" tall, small mirror framed by tiered shelves supported by turned columns, marble over drawer at base, molded and pierced pediment.
**$1,900.00 - 2,250.00**

MARBLE TOP—18″ x 36″

$400.00 - 475.00

* OVAL MARBLE TOP—28″ x 38″, Molded Apron.

$650.00 - 750.00

OVAL MARBLE TOP—26″ x 34″, rosewood, 4 supporting pillars with molded feet, applied molding framing apron with applied ornament.     $850.00 - 900.00

MARBLE TOP—20½″ x 29″, veneered aprons with applied ornaments, drop finials, center urn.

$600.00 - 650.00

*(1876 PRICES: top 18″ x 24″ to 24″ x 32″ — $9.50-13.00)

OVAL MARBLE TOP—26″ x 34″, rosewood, applied molding framing apron, applied ornaments.

**$850.00 - 900.00**

MARBLE TOP—21″ x 30″, 4 supporting pillars with molded feet.

**$500.00 - 550.00**

MARBLE TOP—20″ x 25″

**$375.00 - 425.00**

*OVAL MARBLE TOP—24″ x 38″, burl veneer raised panels on apron and legs, applied ornaments and center urn.

**$550.00 - 650.00**

*(1876 PRICES:  top 18″ x 24″ to 24″ x 32″—$9.50-13.00

*OVAL MARBLE TOP—22″ x 30″, molded legs with applied carving.

**$550.00 - 650.00**

*OVAL MARBLE TOP—22″ x 30″, machine lines on legs, molded apron.

**$450.00 - 500.00**

*OVAL MARBLE TOP—22″ x 30″, simple machine lines on legs, molded apron.

**$500.00 - 550.00**

*OVAL MARBLE TOP—18″ x 22″

**$350.00 - 400.00**

*(1876 PRICES: top 18″ x 24″ to 24″ x 32″—$9.50-13.00)

—RECTANGULAR MARBLE TOP—20″ x 30″, scalloped, burl veneer raised panels on apron and legs, simple applied ornaments and incised lines. **$350.00 - 400.00**

—RECTANGULAR MARBLE TOP—20″ x 30″, burl veneer banding on apron and base, machine lines and carving. **$400.00 - 450.00**

—RECTANGULAR MARBLE TOP—23″ x 32″, burl veneer panels on apron and legs, simple incised lines and carving, burl veneer columns. (Eastlake influence) **$400.00 - 450.00**

—RECTANGULAR MARBLE TOP—23″ x 30″, scalloped corners, burl veneer panels on apron and legs, applied ornaments, incised lines. (Renaissance Revival with Eastlake influence) **$500.00 - 550.00**
—(1876 PRICES—18″ x 25½″ to 20″ x 28½″ — $9.50 - 13.00)

57

—RECTANGULAR MARBLE TOP—20″ x 30″, scalloped corners, simple incised lines, burl veneer banding.
**$300.00 - 350.00**

—RECTANGULAR MARBLE TOP—15″ x 26″, rounded corners, simple incised lines, applied ornaments, center finial.
**$250.00 - 300.00**

—RECTANGULAR MARBLE TOP—22″ x 31″, scalloped corners, burl veneer banding on apron and legs, applied ornaments.
**$375.00 - 400.00**

—RECTANGULAR MARBLE TOP—23″ x 34″, burl veneer panels on apron and legs, drop finials, rounded corners, turned stretcher with urn finial. (Renaissance Revival)
**$450.00 - 500.00**

—(1876 PRICES—18″ x 25½″ to 20″ x 28½″ — $9.50 - 13.00)

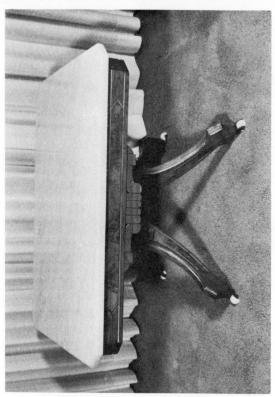

CUT DOWN RECTANGULAR MARBLE TOP—23" x 31", 18" high, burl veneer banding on apron and legs, machine lines and carving. **$200.00 - 250.00**

CUT DOWN OVAL MARBLE TOP—23" x 32", 20" high, molded apron, applied carved ornaments. (Louis XV substyle) **$300.00 - 350.00**

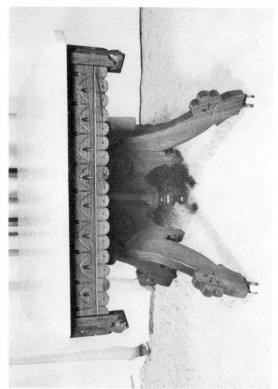

CUT DOWN MARBLE TOP—24" x 24", 19" high, machine incised lines and carving. (Eastlake influence) **$200.00 - 250.00**

CUT DOWN MARBLE TOP—27" x 39", 20" high, applied molding and carving, bottom shelf. (Louis XV substyle) $300.00 - 325.00

CUT DOWN OVAL TOP—26″ x 33″, 19″ high, molded apron.

**$275.00 - 300.00**

OVAL TOP—28″ x 40″

**$350.00 - 400.00**

CUT DOWN RECTANGULAR TOP—20″ x 28″, 20″ high, machine lines and carving, applied ornaments. (Eastlake influence)

**$200.00 - 250.00**

OVAL TOP—24″ x 33″, molded apron.

**$300.00 - 350.00**

OVAL TEAPOY or dressing stand with shelf and one drawer—single turned stretcher.

$100.00 - 125.00

OVAL WORK TABLE—22″ x 29″, turned stretcher

$100.00 - 125.00

OVAL TOP—19″ x 29″, center supporting pillar with stretchers, incised lines and applied ornaments, molded apron.

$300.00 - 350.00

OVAL TOP—20″ x 28″, 5 supporting pillars and molded legs, molded apron.

$250.00 - 300.00

OVAL WORK TABLE—20″ x 33″, shelf-like stretcher
with applied ornament, molded apron.

$125.00 - 150.00

OVAL TOP—17″ x 22″, molded apron.

**$200.00 - 250.00**

*RECTANGULAR TOP—21″ x 29″, legs with supporting
stretchers, incised lines.

**$150.00 - 200.00**

*RECTANGULAR TOP—22″ x 30″, molded apron, single
supporting stretcher with applied ornament.

**$150.00 - 200.00**

*(1876 PRICES—top 18″ x 25½″ -20″ x 28½″ - $4.00 - 9.00)

62

ROUND GAME TABLE—32″ diameter, veneered apron, finials on center of supporting stretchers.

$250.00 - 300.00

RECTANGULAR TOP—21″ x 29″, incised lines.

$150.00 - 175.00

ROUND TABLE—21″ diameter, veneered apron, burl veneer applied panels, applied ornaments.

$250.00 - 300.00

RECTANGULAR TOP—17½″ x 23½″, incised lines, molded apron.

$150.00 - 175.00

RECTANGULAR TOP—21″ x 32″, shelf, incised lines, applied brackets.

$125.00 - 150.00

*RECTANGULAR TOP—21″ x 30″, molded apron, single supporting stretcher, drop finials at corners.

$200.00 - 225.00

*RECTANGULAR TOP—24″ x 36″, scalloped corners, burl veneer panels on legs and stretcher, applied ornaments, molded apron. $250.00 - 275.00

*1876 PRICES—top 18″ x 25½″ - 20″ x 28½″ - $4.00 - 9.00)

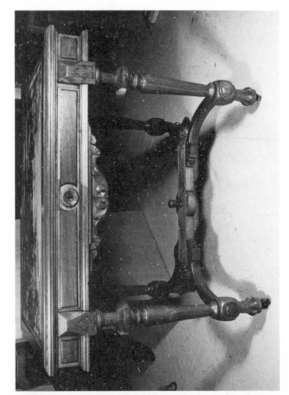

— LIBRARY TABLE—24″ x 40″, applied panels, machine lines and carving, shelf-like supporting stretcher, one drawer. $350.00 - 400.00

-(1876 PRICES—top 26″ x 46″ to 27″ x 52″ — $36.00 - 40.00)

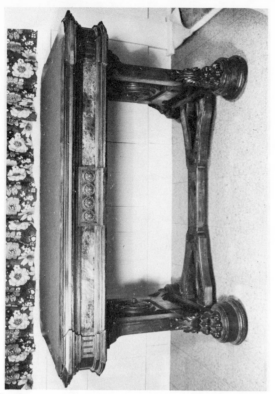

\*LIBRARY TABLE—32″ x 53″, burl veneer panels and banding, applied carved ornaments. **$850.00 - 1,000.00**

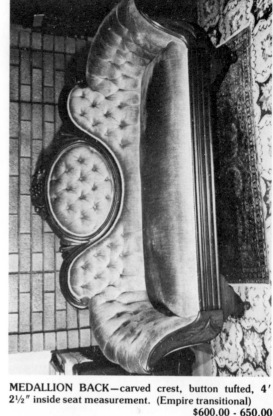

MEDALLION BACK—carved crest, button tufted, 4′ 2½″ inside seat measurement. (Empire transitional)
**$600.00 - 650.00**

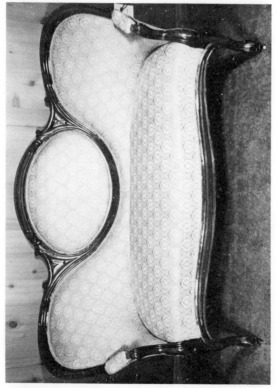

MEDALLION BACK—finger roll, 4′ 2″ inside seat measurement. (Louis XV substyle)

**$550.00 - 650.00**

\*(1876 PRICES—top 26″ x 46″ to 27″ x 52″ — $36.00 - 40.00)

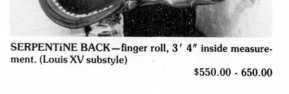

SERPENTiNE BACK—finger roll, 3′ 4″ inside measurement. (Louis XV substyle)

**$550.00 - 650.00**

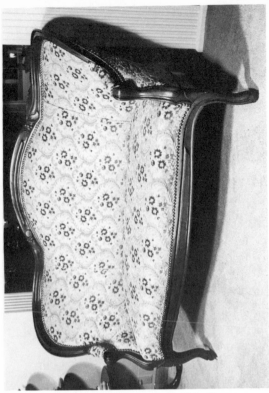

**SERPENTINE BACK**—finger roll, 3′ 6″ inside measurement. (Louis XV substyle)

$550.00 - 650.00

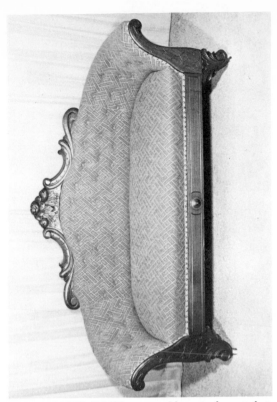

**UPHOLSTERED BACK**—removable carved crest, button tufting, 4′ 5″ inside measurement. (Empire transitional)

$450.00 - 500.00

**FINGER ROLL BACK**—button tufting, 5′ 8″ inside measurement. (Louis XV substyle)

$750.00 - 850.00

**WOODEN FRAMED BACK**—molded crest, applied burl veneer panels, incised lines. (Empire transitional)

$450.00 - 500.00

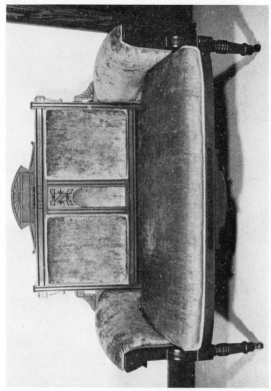

WOODEN FRAMED UPHOLSTERED PANELS—machine lines and carving, burl veneer panels and banding, 3′ 10″ inside measurement. (Eastlake)

$275.00 - 350.00

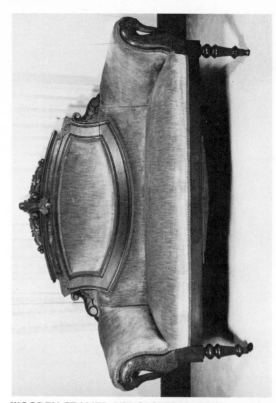

WOODEN FRAMED UPHOLSTERED BACK—molded and paneled crest, incised lines and carving, fowl head molded on arm facings. (Renaissance Revival)

$600.00 - 700.00

STEP BACK SETTEE—machine lines and carving. Overall measurement - 3′. (Eastlake)

$250.00 - 300.00

STEP BACK SETTEE—machine lines and carving. Overall measurement - 3′. (Eastlake)

$250.00 - 300.00

LADY'S CHAIR—button tufting, applied molded carving.

GENTLEMAN'S CHAIR—button tufting, oval back, finger roll, molded carvings on arm supports and crest rail.

GRADUATED DOUBLE ARCH SOFA—button tufting, molded frame, applied carving on apron, finger roll; overall measurement: 6′ 5″. (Louis XV Rococo substyle)

**$2,700.00 - 3,250.00 set**

LADY'S CHAIR—button tufting, burl veneer molded panels, incised lines and carving, applied ornaments, molded crest.

GENTLEMAN'S CHAIR—button tufting, burl veneer molded panels, incised lines and carving, applied ornaments, molded crest.

DOUBLE FRAMED BACK SOFA—button tufting, burl veneer molded panels, incised lines and carving, applied ornaments; overall measurements: 6' 6". (Louis XVI influence)

$2,000.00 - 2,500.00 set

*LAMP STAND—12½" diameter, 34" high, marble recessed in molded rim, tripod base. **$150.00 - 175.00**

*LAMP STAND—19" diameter, 29½" high, marble recessed in molded rim, incised lines, applied ornaments, tripod base. **$250.00 - 300.00**

*LAMP STAND—14" diameter, 32" high, round marble set in recessed molded rim, incised lines, applied ornaments. **$200.00 - 250.00**

*LAMP STAND—16" diameter, 28½" high, marble recessed in molded rim, applied panels and ornaments, tripod base. **$250.00 - 300.00**

*(1876 PRICES—marble top lamp stands - $5.00 - 7.00)

*LAMP STAND—12″ diameter, 32½″ high, round marble set in recessed molded rim, machine lines and carving, carved deer ornament, tripod base. **$350.00 - 400.00**

—LAMP STAND—14½″ diameter, 32½″ high, incised lines on top and legs, tripod base.

**$125.00 - 150.00**

—LAMP STAND—16″ diameter, 28½″ high, incised lines, applied ornaments. **$150.00 - 175.00**

—LAMP STAND—12″ diameter, 29″ high, tripod base
**$100.00 - 125.00**

*(1876 PRICES—marble top lamp stands - $5.00 - 7.00)
—(1876 PRICES—wooden top lamp stands - $4.00 - 6.00)

—LAMP STAND—12″ diameter, 25½ high, incised lines, tripod base.

**$100.00 - 125.00**

*PARLOR STAND—15″ x 20″, marble top, rounded corners, machine lines and carving.

**$200.00 - 250.00**

*PARLOR STAND—15″ x 20″, marble top, squared corners, incised lines, molded apron.

**$175.00 - 200.00**

—(1876 PRICES—wooden top lamp stands - $4.00 - 6.00)

*PARLOR STAND—15″ x 20″, marble top, beveled edge, burl veneer banding on apron and legs

**$225.00 - 250.00**

*(1876 PRICES—parlor stands - $5.00 - 7.00)

\*PARLOR STAND—15″ x 18½″, marble top, beveled edge, burl veneer banding on apron and legs, machine lines, applied ornaments.
**$225.00 - 250.00**

\*PARLOR STAND—15″ diameter, molded apron, incised lines.
**$150.00 - 175.00**

\*PARLOR STAND—16½″ x 22″, marble top, beveled edge, straight front, rounded ends, incised lines.
**$225.00 - 250.00**

\*PARLOR STAND—14″ x 14″, incised lines on top, apron, and legs.

**$75.00 - 100.00**

\*(1876 PRICES—parlor stands - $5.00 - 7.00)

*PARLOR STAND—15″ x 21½″, veneered apron, veneer banding on legs, incised lines.

$225.00 - 250.00

—BOOKCASE—6′ 3″ tall, 3′ 4″ wide, drawers at base, plain front.

$500.00 - 550.00

—BOOKCASE—6′ tall, 4′ wide, burl veneer banding on drawers and cabinet stiles, machine lines and carving, applied ornaments, pierced and paneled gallery.

*(1876 PRICES—parlor stands - 5.00 - 7.00)     $800.00 - 850.00

—BOOKCASE—7′ tall, 4′ wide.  2 drawers at base, plain front.

$450.00 - 500.00

—1876 PRICES—(6′ 50 to 9′ tall and 4′ to 4′ 6″ wide - $20.00 - 48.00)

FOOT STOOL—18″ high, 12″ x 19″ top, incised lines, shelf like stretcher.

$75.00 - 125.00

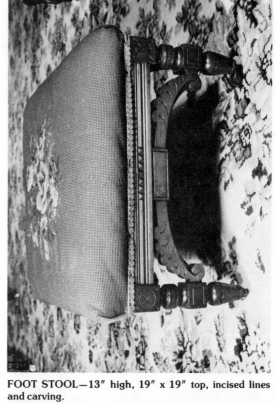

FOOT STOOL—13″ high, 19″ x 19″ top, incised lines and carving.

$75.00 - 125.00

SLIPPER BOX—18″ high, 10″ x 19″ top, incised lines, single turned stretcher. (1876 price for slipper box was $5.00)

$75.00 - 125.00

MAGAZINE RACK—incised lines, chain supported sides.
$100.00 - 125.00

TILT TOP TABLE—32″ diameter, tripod base.
$350.00 - 400.00

GAME TABLE—18″ x 36″, serpentine top, spool legs.
$325.00 - 350.00

GAME TABLE—35″ diameter, applied burl veneer panels, spool legs.
$350.00 - 400.00

GAME TABLE—18″ x 36″, ogee veneered apron.
$225.00 - 275.00

**GAME TABLE**—18″ x 36″, ogee veneered apron, beaded trim, spool legs. (original top missing)

**$200.00 - 225.00**

**GAME TABLE**—18″ x 36″, veneer apron, beading trim.

**$300.00 - 325.00**

# Chapter 5
## Dinner Is Served

In the dining room a table to dine upon, straight chairs, and a storage unit for necessary accessories are the main essentials. In Victorian times, the sideboard (also called buffet) was the dominating feature of the room. Tall creations in walnut were available, and their door panels could be carved with decorative touches such as deceased game fowls hanging upside down or, more pleasantly, with arrangements of fruits and nuts. Panels, moldings, piliasters, and veneering added allure; and a mirror reflected the tea service, cut glass cruet set, candelabrum, or large vases which stood on its surface.

The most inexpensive way to buy a sideboard from a Grand Rapids firm was "in the white" (no finish applied) without marble, pulls, or plate (looking glass), and the recipient could supply any of these extras he desired himself.

The drawers held the necessary silverware which tended to have pronounced patterns flowing with flowers and often with engraved initials. In the 1700's, silver objects were frequently made from coins which were taken to the silversmith to melt down. In the 1830's, silver was sometimes marked pure coin, coin, dollar, or with a C or a D to indicate that, while it was probably not made from melted coins, it had the purity of coin silver, 900 parts pure out of 1000. The stamp sterling indicates 925 purity, a marking found after 1860. Pewter, wood, and pottery were for the poor. Only the wealthy could afford silver products until the process of electroplating over copper or white metal was developed in 1840, and the less expensive plated ware became available. Thus the sideboard became the stage on and in which the new silver products were concentrated.

This impressive furnishing also had drawers for large table cloths of pure Irish linen or of patterned damask complete with their twelve matching napkins. Glass ware and china might also be stored on the shelves inside the sideboard.

The late 1800 sideboard was not so tall as those found in the middle of the period. It was also squarer in its appearance.

The dining table stood in a central place of prominence. Prior to the time of English cabinetmakers Hepplewhite and Sheraton, large ones were rare. During the sphere of their influence (circa 1785-1815 in America) three separate tables were customarily joined to compose one great whole. Usually a rectangle with two fall leaves formed the center. Two tables of corresponding height and width with oval ends stood along the wall. Each could have a rectangular drop leaf. When a number of guests were anticipated, these two consoles could be joined to the central table to make one large version. Presently such a combination is known as a banquet table.

If the family did not own a banquet type, imagine the confusion which could result from pushing tables of slightly different heights and various widths together to form one large continuous surface and you will understand why extension tables were welcomed eagerly when they were introduced in the 1800's.

In the mid-1800's, **Godey's Magazine and Lady's Book** was edited by an intelligent widow with children to support, Sarah Josepha Hale, and she kept women informed about home crafts, the latest fashions, plus current events through such articles as brief biographies about women writers of the day. She also successfully challenged the ladies to complete the monument of Bunker Hill, left unfinished by the males, and wrote "Mary Had a Little Lamb" for tiny tots. In order to keep her readers up-to-date on furniture, she gave them an imaginary tour of the George J. Henkel wareroom at 173 Chestnut St., Philadelphia. Mentioned with enthusiasm was an improved oval extension table with a rope and small windlass mechanism under the rim which permitted it to expand to include additional leaves. Mrs. Hale assured housewives they would be delighted with it. The idea was developed further, and an 1876 furniture list mentions a breakfast table with a "Fall Leaf Patent Extension Frame".

In some forms, one or two additional central legs provided support when the tables were pulled apart for the insertion of extra leaves. On another, a thick columned pedestal base separated in the middle. Stow and Davis of Grand Rapids marketed such a "pillar extension table" in 1887. It was available in oak first, then in walnut and mahogany, at a cost of fifty to seventy five cents a running foot, wholesale. It could stretch out six to twelve feet. A non-extending type was the gate leg with drop leaves and fold in legs. When the leaves were up, the extra legs swung out under them (like a gate moving) to yield support. In many other drop leaves some kind of wooden slides or metal brackets pulled out or flipped up to hold up the leaves. With these innovations groups of diners could be served with ease.

Various chairs might accompany the table. A popular type from around the 1830's through the 1860's was the balloon back with an upholstered seat. An open walnut frame, usually with a carving of a rose or some other natural object at the top, circled out, balloon like, to form the chair back. A slat had a similar motif carved on it. Cabriole legs added to the dainty appearance.

During the Renaissance Revival, straighter lines evolved as crested decorations and turned legs replaced the curved Louis XV gentleness. Both the back and seats could be upholstered. The Eastlake influence continued the rectangular look after 1870.

In less formal surroundings, cane chairs were found, some of which featured both a woven seat and back of this flexible rattan. Rungs (stretchers) running between the legs gave additional support; and some people like to imagine that the front stretcher which bows in is a "hoop skirt rung" because they feel its shape helped accommodate the yards and yards of fabric the long-skirted ladies wore. However, if a female sat on that under hoop, which made her dress stand out all the way around, it would raise up in the front; and since this exposure would not be proper or graceful, a belle learned to lift and squeeze the rearward rings slightly, then back into a sitting position being careful to sit on the cloth only. It was easier to avoid chairs with arms or to select those with abbreviated versions when there were bouncing hoops and so much dress material to spread out and keep unwrinkled as one sat.

When not caned, backs could have splats running vertically, but the most common kind had slats which ran horizontally. The top one might be ornamented with carving or small pieces of veneer which formed a design or feature a combination of both. Painted examples were considered "cottage furniture" and are not treated here.

Seats could be round, semi-circular in front, or almost square. Chairs of this type could be used with a dining table, be kitchen mates, or serve as additional seats wherever needed.

Cupboards for storage could be placed in the dining room, and if the setting was fancy, so were the cabinets. On a breakfront, the center projects out a little further than the ends which form the top and base. This breaks the straight line of the front to give the piece its descriptive name. Often glass doors above showed off the family's Haviland or Spode while the base portion had drawers plus wooden doors. In addition some cupboards came in two pieces and a small shelf might be formed in the space between the two units. Cornices could be plain or elaborate. Carved pulls, molding, and veneering added decorative touches.

The Victorian dining room was the site of leisurely entertaining with feasting and pleasant conversation, and so naturally the furnishings were expected to be attractive and comfortable.

**DINING TABLE**—rectangular drop leaf, 21″ x 44″, 16″ drop leaves.

$225.00 - 250.00

**DINING TABLE**—rectangular extension, 30″ x 42″, incised lines, applied ornaments, applied brackets.

$175.00 - 200.00

**DINING TABLE**—retangular extension, 30″ x 42″, incised lines.

$175.00 - 200.00

**DINING TABLE**—extension drop leaf, 28″ x 42″, 14½″ drop leaves.

$200.00 - 225.00

DINING TABLE—square extension 48″ x 48″, pedestal base, incised lines, veneer panels on apron and base.

$800.00 - 900.00

DINING TABLE—rectangular gate leg drop leaf, 21″ x 44½″, 19½″ drop leaves.

$400.00 - 450.00

DINING TABLE—oval drop leaf extension, 23″ x 41″, 14″ drop leaves.

$175.00 - 200.00

DINING TABLE—round extension, 48″ diameter, pedestal base, applied burl veneer panels, applied ornaments.

$950.00 - 1,250.00

**DINING TABLE**—oval drop leaf extension with supporting center leg, 23″ x 41″, 14″ drop leaves.

**$300.00 - 375.00**

**DINING TABLE**—square extension, 48″ x 48″, pedestal base, machine lines and carving, applied ornaments.

**$800.00 - 900.00**

**CUPBOARD**—7′ 2″ tall, 4′ 8″ wide, door panels framed by applied molding.

**$1,250.00 - 1,500.00**

**CUPBOARD**—6′ 10″ tall, 3′ 6″ wide, recessed top, plain front.

**$600.00 - 700.00**

CUPBOARD—6' 4" tall, 3' 10" wide, recessed top, applied molding around glass and carved pulls, projection front.
**$750.00 - 800.00**

SIDEBOARD—7' 7" tall, 5' wide, marble top, burl veneer panels, machine lines and carving, applied ornaments. (Eastlake)
**$1,500.00 - 1,600.00**

SIDEBOARD—7' tall, 5' wide, marble top, applied circular molding, applied burl veneer panels, applied carving and ornaments, rounded ends. (Renaissance Revival)
**$2,250.00 - 2,500.00**

SIDEBOARD—6' 9", tall, 5' 6" wide, marble top, burl veneer banding, machine lines and carving, applied ornaments, machine carved gallery. (Eastlake)
**$1,400.00 - 1,600.00**

SIDEBOARD—3′ 1″ tall, 3′ 6″ wide, circular molding, burl veneer applied panels, molded drawer frames.
$425.00 - 525.00

SIDEBOARD—6′ 4″ tall, 4′ wide, applied molding framing drawers and doors, applied ornaments and carving, applied swags, molded pediment, incised lines. (Renaissance Revival with Eastlake influence) $1,000 - 1,200

SIDEBOARD—6′ 11″ tall, 4′ 6″ wide, marble top, circular molding, applied panels, applied ornaments and carving, applied swags, molded pediment. (Renaissance Revival)
$1,600.00 - 1,800.00

SIDEBOARD—8′ tall, 5′ 9″ wide, marble top, applied molding on drawers and doors, applied burl veneer panels, applied ornaments and carving, rounded ends, molded pediment, deer head. (Renaissance Revival)
$2,250.00 - 2,500.00

SIDEBOARD—7' 1" tall, 4' 3" wide, marble top, molded drawers with burl veneer panels, raised and recessed burl veneer panels in upper section, chamfered corner stiles with applied molding and panels, projection front. (Renaissance Revival with Eastlake influence)

$1,100 - 1,300

SIDEBOARD—6' 6" tall, 4' wide, marble top, molded door frames with veneer panels and applied carving, applied burl veneer panels, carving and ornaments, molded pediment, fluted corner stiles. (Renaissance Revival)

**$1,500.00 - 1,700.00**

SIDEBOARD—7' 3" tall, 4' 7" wide, marble top, applied molding framing drawers and doors, applied burl veneer panels, turned columns supporting shelf, veneered doors, drawers and rounded corner stiles, elablorately molded and carved pediment with swag. (Renaissance Revival)

**$1,800.00 - 2,200.00**

SIDEBOARD—8' tall, 4' wide, marble top, recessed burl veneer panels, machine lines and carving, applied ornaments and panels. (Eastlake)

$750.00 - 950.00

CANE CHAIR—cane back arm chair, square seat, machine lines and carving.

$125.00 - 150.00

CANE CHAIR—round cane seat, demi-arms, applied burl veneer panels, slat back.

Set of 4:   $135.00 - 150.00 each

CANE CHAIR—demi-arm chair, applied burl veneer, slat back. (formerly caned seat)

$175.00 - 225.00

CANE CHAIR—square cane seat, demi-arms, burl veneer banding, incised lines, splat back.

Set of 4:   $125.00 - 150.00 each

CANE CHAIR—round cane seat, demi-arms, burl veneer trim, incised lines, splat back.

**Set of 4:  $125.00 - 150.00 each**

CANE CHAIR—round cane seat, demi-arms, veneer trim, incised lines, splat back.

**Set of 4:  $125.00 - 150.00 each**

CANE CHAIR—U shaped cane seat, demi-arms, burl veneer trim, slat and spindle back.

**Set of 4:  $125.00 - 150.00 each**

CANE CHAIR—square cane seat and back, demi-arms, veneer trim, machine lines and carving.

**Set of 4:  $150.00 - 175.00 each**

CANE CHAIR—round cane seat, demi-arms, applied ornaments, splat back, finger hole in top rail.

**Set of 4: $150.00 - 175.00 each**

CANE CHAIR—round cane seat, burl veneer trim, incised lines, splat back.

**Set of 4: $125.00 - 150.00 each**

CANE CHAIR—round cane seat and U shaped back, demi-arms, burl veneer trim, incised lines, applied ornaments.

**Set of 4: $200.00 - 225.00 each**

CANE CHAIR—square cane seat, slat back, flat front rung.

**Set of 4: $100.00 - 125.00 each**

CANE CHAIR—square cane seat, slat back, concave front rung.

**Set of 4: $100.00 - 125.00 each**

CANE CHAIR—round cane seat, spindle back.

**Set of 4: $150.00 - 175.00 each**

CANE CHAIR—U shaped cane seat, incised carving, slat back.

**Set of 4: $100.00 - 125.00 each**

CANE CHAIR—needle point over cane seat, carved crest, slat back, concave front rung, finger hole, serpentine front.

**Set of 4: $100.00 - 125.00 each**

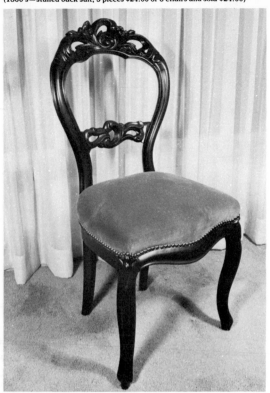

**BALLOON BACK, FINGER ROLL SIDE CHAIR**—carved crest. (Louis XV)

**$200.00 - 225.00**

**BALLOON BACK, FINGER ROLL SIDE CHAIR**— carved crest, tufted seat. (Louis XV)

**$225.00 - 250.00**

**BALLOON BACK, FINGER ROLL SIDE CHAIR**— carved crest. (Louis XV)

**$200.00 - 225.00**

**BALLOON BACK, FINGER ROLL SIDE CHAIR**— carved crest. (Louis XV)

**$225.00 - 250.00**

**SLIP SEAT SIDE CHAIR**—Empire Transitional, carved crest, serpentine apron.

$175.00 - 200.00

**BALLOON BACK, FINGER ROLL SIDE CHAIR**—demi-arms. (Louis XV)

$150.00 - 175.00

**SIDE CHAIR**—Empire transitional, slat back, serpentine apron.

$150.00 - 175.00

**BALLOON BACK, FINGER ROLL SIDE CHAIR**—demi-arms. (Louis XV)

$175.00 - 200.00

# Chapter 6
## The Heart of the Home

There are always slogans which declare that guests like the kitchen best, and Victorians, who were considered sentimentalists, would probably have agreed that the kitchen is the heart of the home. Often, in ordinary households, a woman had a small rocker in which she sat as she shelled peas, took the strings off beans, peeled apples for pies or sauce, pared potatoes, or performed other essential tasks connected with feeding her family. Cane, plank seated, or rush chairs could be included in the kitchen decor. Naturally, work tables and a breakfast table were essentials, and since shelves were not built-in features, kitchen cabinets and cupboards were vital.

Cupboards come in many versions from early ones with panels to later styles with framed glass which exposed the contents to view. When glass was first used, small panes were framed with wood to make a door because glass was a luxury item blown by human lung power and was not available in large sheets. For two thousand years the process changed little until a carpenter, Enoch Robinson, suggested, circa 1825, that instead of hand blowing the molten glass into molds, why not ladle the hot liquid and press it into shape with a plunger? He constructed wooden molds and his tests proved successful. Gradually glass, which once only the wealthy could own, became a mass produced product inexpensive enough for the commoner to purchase and place in his home. Maybe that's why matrons in the 1800's enjoyed tall mirrors and glass encased cupboards and bookcases. These, plus all the glass babbles and pressed table wares, represented something new.

When wooden panels are found in storage units, many times they are removed and replaced with glass or wire backed with glass is inserted to please the present-day housewife.

A pie safe formed a haven from mice and flies where home baked goods could be stored. The majority of homemakers, without the aid of instant mixes, baked bread in large batches. Pies were not made singly and cakes might be in triplicate to feed the family with its large number of children plus the hired hands. Rodents and flies were annoying problems, and to deter their activities, sweets were stored in this special cabinet. Commonly it had sides and front panels of pierced tin. The holes were punched in such a manner as to create a design such as stars, hearts, or geometric patterns, but on rare occasions an artistic soul took over and created a senic view or animals, but these are rare and command a greater price than the more prosaic themes. The metal kept out the undesirables and yet the perforations allowed air to circulate to help keep the contents free from mold.

Other small varieties are dubbed jelly cupboards today, and these are usually functional and plain. Ventilation was provided in many examples by open work cut into the wood in circles or other designs. Screening covered these holes on the inside and kept pests out.

Corner cupboards were triangular in shape and, as the name implies, were backed into corners where they fit snugly. Pine and poplar examples are frequent, but hardwood versions are found on occasion.

Naturally, cupboards varied in designs. Some were constructed as a single unit and were straight up and down while others had a base with a series of shelves set on top to form a two-piece unit. The base might jut out further than the upper shelves.

White procelain or wooden handles appeared early and cast metal types were later. The catch to hold the doors closed might be a small plug of wood which pivoted on a central screw.

Even though built-ins are prevalent today, people who enjoy antiques acquire cupboards to place throughout the house. Books and bric-a-brac, collections, kitchen ware, games, or linens can be stored inside. In a youth's bedroom, cumbersome garments such as bulky jeans and sweatshirts can be seen immediately without unnecessary pawing through when a cabinet door is opened. Because of their versatility, the nineteenth century cupboards retain their popularity.

One item for a tiny child might be found in the kitchen area—the high chair. A place to sleep and a place to eat in comparative comfort and safety—these are two prime requisites on the list of accessory items for infants.

In the late 1800's Victorians were intrigued by combination furniture, and many ideas were patented. A bed wardrobe or a bookcase desk unit were acceptable, but what else could a high chair become? One version can be collapsed into a cradle to take care of both the eating and sleeping requirements while, with the release of a lock, certain types may be lowered to form rocking chairs. Others have small wheels and can convert into stroller-type buggies, and some include several such features.

Often high chairs had removable trays so that they could serve as youth chairs after the baby crossed into childhood but was still too small to reach the table comfortably. Of course, there were always versions with splayed legs for a safety feature with either a plank or cane seat and back which functioned for one purpose only—a safe eating spot for baby.

It's difficult to decide where a daybed should be located, but sometimes such a bed was placed in the kitchen area so that a farmer home from the fields could flop down for a few moment's rest while his wife, the hired girl, and his daughters finished dinner preparations. From usage such as this it received its name.

A daybed is an overgrown chair with a series of legs, its style, carvings, and turnings conforming with the pattern of chairs popular in the period when it was produced. The seat is long enough to permit a person to sprawl out, full length, for a quickly snatched snooze. Often there is an adjustable back rest for those who prefer to recline daintily. Known as long ago as ancient Greek and Roman days, it was probably the first "sofa" type introduced to Europe in about 1680. When the machine age hit the United States, the public began to demand mass production of inexpensive furniture and manufacturers were delighted to oblige. Country spool (or spindled) furniture was one result. Price lists from the 1870's might refer to these narrow beds as lounges.

Some of these rest beds (and regular size frames as well) have a loose end rail which swivels in its socket. This was a "done on purpose" construction to accommodate an extra cover which could be rolled off the blanket rail if the occupant grew chilly and required additional warmth.

Many daybeds had a dual function as there were two additional inner legs which could be pulled out to expose a slat-filled frame. This gave added resting space since, with padding placed over it, it could almost be the grandaddy of a modern sofa bed. Today when toss back pillows are used to add comfort to the sitter, these can be made the same size as the pulled-out section so that they can be a mattress should the bed be required to sleep extra guests.

This pull-out variety might be called a "hired man's bed" as it could offer a sleeping place for a farm hand in a room under sloping eaves. Backless versions called window seats might be placed in window alcoves and a sitter would have "double vision" since he could see what was happening both inside the house and out, and this type could appear in the sitting room.

Naturally there are many pieces which are difficult to classify by special rooms. In an average home much grooming was done in the kitchen back in the days when water for washing or bathing had to be hauled in from outside in pails and heated on the big black wood or coal burning stove. Some ranges were handy because they contained a reservoir for keeping water warm. A man's shaving stand could be in the kitchen so he could readily dip out heated water or pour some from a teakettle into a basin in order to shave. A large wooden tub pulled out and placed in the middle of the kitchen floor became a bathtub on Saturday nights and each member of the family took a turn sitting in it to scrub himself clean with hunks of homemade soft soap. A wash bowl and pitcher, a walnut hanging comb case and mirror were standard equipment in an average kitchen.

CANE HIGH CHAIR with swing out tray.
$225.00 - 250.00

HIGH CHAIR, collapes to a stroller.
$250.00 - 275.00

WINDOW SEAT with blanket rolls, spindle ends, 4′ 9½″
(also called day bed or hired man's bed)
$275.00 - 300.00

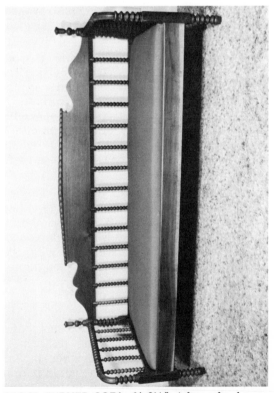

SPOOL TURNED SOFA, 6′ 2½″, (often refered to as
Jenny Lind day bed)
$275.00 - 325.00

PIE SAFE with pierced tin, 4′ 5″ high, 14″ x 39½″ top.
$350.00 - 400.00

FOOD SAFE with triangular cut our air vents on sides, 5′ high, 3′ 7″ wide.
$300.00 - 350.00

CUPBOARD, 7′ 1″ high, 3′ 3″ wide, plain front.
$400.00 - 450.00

CUPBOARD, 6′ 6″ high, 3′ 10″ wide, plain front.
$450.00 - 500.00

# Chapter 7
## Climb into Bed

It has been estimated that about one third of a person's life is spent in bed. During the past century, hospitals did not have the prominence they do today. Babies were born in the home and physicians administered assistance to the ill in their own bedrooms. Thus, the bed sheltered both life and death.

The furnishings of the room depended on the social status of the family, but basically consisted of a three piece matching set with a bed, some sort of a chest of drawers probably with an attached mirror since mirrors were not fastened to the walls then, and a commode to hold supplies which were necessary for sanitation and washing in a day when indoor plumbing was not common. Since closets usually were not built in, wardrobes in which clothes could be hung were handy, but otherwise hooks along the walls could suffice.

In more elaborate rooms, a fireplace might be present and an easy chair would be available to pull up to its warmth. Other comfortable additions might include straight chairs, small lamp tables, dressing stands, and possibly a full length mirror in a standing frame.

You are invited to come along and examine Victorian walnut bedroom furniture as found in the chambers of a nineteenth century home.

What's a bed?

Formerly this word referred to a feather mattress which was placed on a frame called a bedstead. Feather beds often rested on interlaced heavy rope tightened about knobs spaced equal distance in the wooden side, head, and food rails which were usually round. Frames such as this were made in the 1800's and now are called "rope beds".

Where did the phrase "climb into bed originate"?

Bedsteads from the past were made high off the floor and when a mattress was placed on top of them, the sleeping surface was even higher. Sometimes it was necessary to have a few steps nearby so that someone could literally "climb into bed" because of the height off the floor. Possibly that it how the phrase came to be.

One simple early 1800's bedstead had spool turnings. These resembled spools, buttons, or knobs placed in a row and were used in furniture in the 1820's remaining around until the 1870's. When showman Phineas T. Barnum promoted an American tour for singer Jenny Lind, the "Swedish Nightingale", in 1850-52, men in some cities removed her horses and pulled her carriage through the streets themselves. She was immortalized by the glass factories in pattern glass, merchandise was named in her honor, and since spool bedsteads were modish at that time, they have come to be called "Jenny Lind beds". Curved posts (round corners, an old catalog says) are more difficult to turn on a lathe than straight ones, so the straight type are earlier. Generally, hardwoods such as cherry, walnut, or most commonly maple, were replaced by pine in spool bedsteads from the middle of the century on. However, this is not true in a Grand Rapids catalog of the 1870's which offers maple round corner spindled bedsteads for sale. Although the illustration shows the Jenny Lind style, there is no mention of spool turnings or of the Swedish singer's name. Since spool furniture was not expensive, many families could afford this style and it represents almost a country-type furniture.

Another famous woman who lived in the 1800's was social worker Jane Addams who founded Hull House. When he met her, the Russian author Count Nikolayevich Tolstoi, who renounced his wealth to serve God among the peasants, expressed surprise that Jane Addams could work in Chicago slums and dress in the manner in which she did. Why didn't she wear simplier, skimpier garments which required less fabric and clothe others in the remnants? The Count should have seen her back in 1876 when Miss Addams was sixteen. Then a fashionable woman's floor-sweeping dress was extremely plump requiring yards of material with exotic ones possibly utilizing over thirty-five yards of goods.

A similar exuberance was seen in the construction of ornately carved Renaissance Revival bedsteads which stretched ceilingward over eight feet. So ponderous were some of these frames that someone has suggested it would be possible to conserve wood and construct an entire bedstead out of one of the thick heavy side rails.

One massive oak frame which won an award at the Centennial Exposition in Philadelphia in 1876 commemorated the one hundredth birthday of the United States in a symbolic way. A wooden eagle spread his wings out from the topmost position, and niches held statuettes which flanked the bed with Washington in the middle at the head and Columbia at the foot. Columbus was also represented as were about six others, and the Nelson, Matter Company just happened to have this creation in the stock room. Their historian maintains they did not make it up special for the occasion. Other Grand Rapids firms which won awards at this exhibition which featured industrial, art, and craft displays from some fifty countries were Berkey & Gay and the Phoenix Furniture Co.

Berkey & Gay sent a "chamber suit" consisting of a black walnut bed and a marble top dressing case with a matching commode. It was purchased the following year as a wedding present for seven thousand dollars and is now on display at the Grand Rapids Museum. The location of the Nelson, Matter bed which sold for three thousands dollars at the Exposition is unknown. It's disappeared.

Grand Rapids could produce exotic bedsteads because various wood carvers who learned their trade working in the shipyards in Glasgow, Scotland, came to the United States. They had chipped out figure heads for ships, made decorations from stem to stern, and added woodwork to cabins of all types of vessels. Their deft chisels carved delicately.

Half-tester bedsteads, with tall posts and a canopy or tester extending over the head of the frame only, date to around the 1860's and before. This style was especially popular in the South and is a carry over from a time when draperies helped protect sleepers from drafts as well as from the dreaded night air which was considered poisonous.

One owner of a large Renaissance bedstead proudly stated that she and her husband bought cast-offs when they were married after the Second World War because factories had been putting out necessary war materials. When they reconverted for peacetime production, the quality of their merchandise was poor and prices were high; therefore the newly weds sought nineteenth century furniture which was inexpensive yet had quality.

About fifteen years ago (circa 1960's) second hand stores priced the overpowering beds of the late 1800's in the under twenty dollars category. They seldom attracted customers. People who bought them at auction paid only a few dollars and frequently cut them up for lumber in order to repair other pieces. Many bedsteads met this fate as they did not fit into small homes and could not qualify even as give away items. A ninety-five-year-old woman recalls that her mother wanted new styles so when metal beds were modish in the late 1800's, out went the walnut superstructures to be chopped up and burned.

Currently young people are buying and restoring run-down huge vintage houses and are seeking large antiques which can not be placed in modern homes with eight foot ceilings. Now the beds are coming out of retirement but they are not so plentiful as they were. Scarcity and demand have zoomed their prices to a peak point.

In walnut, the period terminated with Eastlake's straight lined bed frames which were available in the 1870's. Some of these could be ornate with carvings and panels.

An 1876 price list shows a maple round corner panel bed which was available in single or three fourth sizes for the same price. It sold for two dollars and seventy five cents in white (no finish added) and three dollars and forty cents finished light or dark. Therefore, bedsteads came in three sizes—double, three fourths, and single, but twin beds (two singles which matched) were not popular until the twentieth century. Sizes termed three quarter because of their sparse dimensions were numerous, however. While it is possible to have a mattress made today to fit such beds, special rails usually are inserted to accommodate a standard size. The original rails should be retained if one desires to keep the piece authentic, and they can be stored in the garage, perhaps.

Another bedroom essential is a storage space for clothes. In France, a bureau signifies a desk, but in the United States it is a bedroom chest of drawers where clothes are kept. A tall narrow kind may be called a chiffonier (spelled cheffonier in a nineteenth century catalog). In the Nelson, Matter & Co. price list of January 1st, 1873, three piece "Chamber Suits" included a bed, bureau, and a washstand which might be either a three drawer bureau washstand or a commode type with a drawer and two doors. The customer could buy any article or all three. Options included such features as marble, plate, handles, urns on the bedposts; and suits were offered with or without finish. "In the white" indicated that no finish was applied but an additional four dollar charge per set included this service. If a bureau were ordered without a plate, it would be minus a looking glass, the plate of glass. A projecting front meant that the top drawer had an overhang. The romance is gone from sleuthing to seek an apron which is actually the front of a concealed drawer. It wasn't a secret hiding place for treasures years ago. Instead, it was a repository for slippers and was a "slipper drawer".

A selection of sixteen carved pulls was available, and various "toilets" were shown. "Toilet" was a term which referred to grooming, hence a toilet is a mirror. The mirrors came in various sizes and styles and while some swung in their frames, others were stationary. Versions with an oval shape were tagged "oval", but currently the wishbone shape of the frame causes them to be called "wishbone mirrors". Sometimes boxes with hinged tops which sat on the bureau were joined to the detachable mirror frame. Naturally, the cheapest way to buy a bureau would be "in the white", with no handles or plate, and these "chamber suits" could also be considered "bureau suits".

In its March 1st, 1876 price list, the company refers to "Dressing Case suits". A dressing case had a tall mirror which almost seemed to stretch from floor to ceiling plus a heavily carved walnut frame which could include two small stands, seemingly a logical place to put candlesticks so that milady could see to preen and a gentleman could caress his mustache. Two small drawers were situated on either side which could store small articles such as jewelry. They could be topped with marble or wood, and the surface of the well in between them would be treated to match. Two long low drawers would comprise the base. Veneers, moldings, panels, and carvings added ornamentation. Presently shops call these dressing cases well or step down dressers, both of which are descriptive terms. Some are massive and highly decorated.

The matching commode washstand was utilized to hold a chamber set and served as a place to wash and groom back when bathrooms did not exist in the ordinary home. This case piece came in various styles, and the daintier items from a toilet set (such as the soap dish, toothbrush holder, and cold water pitcher) might be placed on the surface. In the commode washstand there could be one or two full drawers across the top to hold towels, wash cloths, and grooming aids, with two doors beneath which opened to expose space for the slop jar, wash basin and large pitcher. (Usually the chamber pot was modestly hidden under the bed, ready for a quick draw in time of need. It was a daily housekeeping chore to dump its contents in the privy and cleanse it.) Others consisted of a full drawer with two smaller drawers beneath on one half and one door which opened to display storage shelves. Sometimes there was a small hole cut in the side underneath the top with a retractable rod which could be extended to hold towels and wash cloths.

The wooden rail or gallery at the rear was frequently classified as a splash back because it helped keep water from hitting the wall when someone who liked to splatter washed. Some rails included a miniature shelf to hold a soap dish. Marble tops and marble splash backs were desirable sophisticates and could be obtained in low back or high back forms with two shelves and brackets.

Stands with fake drawers which could have tops which lifted up to reveal a well for the wash bowl and pitcher are known as lift-top commodes. At times the production cost was lowered when the sides were made of base wood stained to match the rest or a less desirable wood could be colored and grained to resemble a more expensive contemporary. Ebony and gilt drop pulls (called tear drops currently), round knobs, carved wooden or composition pulls, or ornamental backplates with brass drops (bales) were utilized. Decorative touches included carvings, applied turnings, or fancy veneers.

A petite stand with one drawer, a marble top, and door beneath with shelves inside is known as a commode in today's vocabulary. This beside table is labeled a "somnoe" in an 1876 Grand Rapids furniture catalog.

Small three drawer chests which were called bureau washstands have a "use me almost anywhere" quality. They can hold linens in the bathroom or dining area, grace a hallway, or be placed, instead of an end table, near a sofa in the living room. Once they were pretty much relegated to the bedroom.

Older versions have the solid plank sides while later styles may have a panel (framed) type. Quality pieces are made completely of sought after woods of the period such as walnut or cherry, but less expensive versions may have a wood considered less desirable stained to resemble the choice lumber. Many have a back rail or splash back.

Marble tops carry a premium stamp. In contour the top should match the chest itself. A high or low back rail (with or without small built-in stands, perhaps for the soap dish) is common on both marble and wooden tops. If one were intended but is absent, its loss can be detected because there will be an inch or so of space at the rear of the chest top.

Infrequently, there may be two small drawers parallel to each other with two long drawers beneath. These four drawers are much less common than three drawer versions. Distinct too are the types with the towel bars at each end and the ones with a retractable rod, both of which are not as frequently available.

Common washstands (the English call them "wash-hand stands") were produced around 1840 and continued to be made for use in rural areas up until the early years of the twentieth century. A Victorian version, a stand with towel bars at each end, one drawer with a shelf below, was ordinarily a bedroom piece for washing hands and faces with water carried from the well or pumped from the cistern. The type with a hole in the center into which a basin was placed is not as readily found as the solid top variety.

Today these stands function well as bedside or sofa tables, as bathroom units, or as plant stands. (Protect their surface from water, however.) They're dainty enough to be congenial 'most any place.

When closets were not included in house construction, bedrooms needed a storage unit for clothes, and the Victorians seemed to like theirs massive when they purchased wardrobes. If you are enamored with French words, it becomes an armoire. (Originally this meant a cupboard where arms or unweildy armor was stored.) There could be a division with shelves and a deep drawer on one side and a clothes press (a space to hang garments) on the other. Possibly a wide drawer or two parallel ones would be provided at the base.

Because this was a bulky piece of furniture, ingenious craftsmen made versions which could be collapsed completely by removing pegs. The sides, back, doors, and shelves would then be easy to transport as separate units and could be reassembled elsewhere.

These wardrobes have come out of retirement to function as intended or to store such things as games in recreation rooms. When armoires are converted into gun cabinets, they are serving in a modern interpretation of their original function.

There were other miscellaneous furnishings which could be found in bedrooms. Some have a stable sound. For example, what's the connection between a horse and a looking glass? "Horse" in French is "cheval", and a mirror mounted on swivels in a frame so that it can be tilted is called a cheval mirror. Hence, in this sense, "cheval" suggests a support or frame in which the looking glass swings.

Commonly such a mirror stands on the floor and is long enough to reveal the full figure. However, the term can include small ones which are made to be placed on a table or chest and often this latter type has a drawer between the posts. These petite versions may be referred to as dressing or toilet mirrors while the tall type may be termed a robing glass.

And here's another barn sound. The English call them "towel horses", but on this side of the Atlantic the wooden frames upon which towels can be hung are referred to as towel racks. Made from about the 1750's onward, they were frequently of walnut, and with their rails filled with terry cloth in coordinated colors they are attractive accessory items in the bathrooms of today.

Dealers dub larger sizes blanket racks. With vibrant folk art quilts in quaint patterns draped on them, they are bright additions to the bedroom decor.

For lighting, a small rectangular table with turned legs served as a lamp holder. For dressing, a shaving stand was a small table with an adjustable mirror which a man could use when he shaved. It originated in the late 1600's and was further developed by the Victorians. Some incorporated a basin. There were also "toilet stands", referring to grooming tables where women might sit to comb their hair and primp.

A reclining upholstered piece, now termed a "fainting couch", would be found in some Victorian bedrooms. An 1873 price list describes it merely as a "couch". It featured an extended chairlike structure with a built-in pillow rest for the back, and the long seat provided room for one to stretch out her legs. This "chaise longue" kind of furnishing promised relaxation. It came with or without a back, and while there were rather plain versions, others had wooden frames with serpentine lines, crested carvings, and the anticipated Victorian exuberance for ornamentation. However, the basic ingredient needed in a chamber was a bed, and after the towering Renaissance specimens, Eastlake's influence with its squatter and squarer lines represented a decided change. A Grand Rapids 1876 price list mentions an "Ash East Lake Suit" so in less than ten years after the publication of his book on furniture styles, Charles Lock Eastlake's influence had spread across the Atlantic from England to America's mid-west. Even though the manufacturer managed to misspell his name, the architect-writer's designs were known.

CHAISE LONGUE—5′ 10″ long, incised lines and carving. (Eastlake)
**$350.00 - 400.00**

CHAISE LONGUE—5′ 2″ long, finger roll. (Louis XV)
$600.00 - 700.00

(1876 PRICES—$9.00 - 13.00)

100

\* COMMON WASHSTAND—with towel bars, top 17″ x 26″.

$200.00 - 250.00

\* COMMON WASHSTAND—with towel bars, top 15″ x 21″.

$200.00 - 250.00

\* COMMON WASHSTAND—with towel bars, top 17″ x 26″, serpentine front.

$225.00 - 275.00

WASHSTAND—top 16½″ x 27½″.

$135.00 - 165.00

\*(1876 PRICES—top 16″ x 20″ and 16″ x 28″ - $2.40 - 2.75)

101

**WASHSTAND WITH HOLE FOR WASH BASIN**—top
16″ x 33″.

**$250.00 - 275.00**

— **LAMP TABLE**—top 20″ x 22″

**$175.00 - 200.00**

\* **WASHSTAND**—top 18″ x 30″

**$175.00 - 225.00**

— **LAMP TABLE**—top 22″ x 22″

**$150.00 - 175.00**

\*(1876 PRICES—top 18″ x 30″ - 1.90)

—(1876 PRICE—top 18″ x 18″ - 1.50)

— LAMP TABLE—top 19″ x 22″

**$150.00 - 175.00**

DROP LEAF SEWING STAND—top 15½″ x 22″, 9″ drops.

**$175.00 - 200.00**

— LAMP TABLE—top 20″ x 22″

**$150.00 - 175.00**

—(1876 PRICE—top 18″ x 18″ - 1.50)

DROP LEAF SEWING STAND—top 17″ x 22″, 9″ drops.

**$300.00 - 350.00**

DROP LEAF SEWING STAND—top 18″ x 24″, 11″ drops.

$175.00 - 225.00

SEWING STAND—top 16″ x 24″, applied burl veneer panel.

$275.00 - 325.00

SEWING STAND—top 16″ x 22½″, applied molding framing drawers, trestle supported shelf.

$200.00 - 250.00

SEWING STAND—top 16″ x 22″.

$175.00 - 200.00

WORK TABLE—top 18" x 28", spool legs.
$175.00 - 200.00

WORK TABLE—top 17" x 34", spool legs.
$200.00 - 225.00

WORK TABLE—top 18" x 22½", scalloped corners.
$125.00 - 150.00

COMMODE WASHSTAND—marble top with towel rods, molded burl veneer panels on drawers and door, fluted corner stiles.
$450.00 - 500.00

COMMODE WASHSTAND—marble top, burl banding on drawers, burl veneer panels on doors, carving, molded pilasters, projection front. **$600.00 - 650.00**

COMMODE WASHSTAND—marble top, applied burl veneer panels on drawer and doors. **$500.00 - 550.00**

COMMODE WASHSTAND—marble top, applied burl veneer panels on drawer and doors, rounded corner stiles. **$500.00 - 550.00**

COMMODE WASHSTAND—marble top, molded burl veneer panels on drawer and doors, applied molded ornaments on corner stiles and drawer front. **$500.00 - 550.00**

**COMMODE WASHSTAND**—marble top, molded drawer and doors with applied burl veneer panels.

$500.00 - 550.00

**COMMODE WASHSTAND**—marble top with high splash back and soap shelves, applied burl veneer panel on drawer, applied ornaments on corner stiles.

$550.00 - 600.00

**COMMODE WASHSTAND**—marble top with high splash back and soap shelves, molded burl veneer panels on drawer, doors, and camfered corner stiles, applied molding framing drawer and doors.

$650.00 - 700.00

**COMMODE WASHSTAND**—marble top with high splash back and soap shelves, applied circular molding on drawer and doors, applied burl veneer panel on drawer, rounded corner stiles.

$650.00 - 700.00

107

COMMODE WASHSTAND—wooden top with splash back, molded burl veneer panels on drawer and doors, applied carved molding on corner stiles. **$300.00 - 350.00**

COMMODE WASHSTAND—wooden top with splash back, applied circular molding on doors.

**$350.00 - 400.00**

COMMODE WASHSTAND—marble top with high splash back and soap shelves, applied burl veneer panels on drawer, doors, and upper corner stiles, carved molding on lower corner stiles. **$650.00 - 700.00**

COMMODE WASHSTAND—wooden top with splash back, applied circular molding on drawer, applied ornaments on corner stiles, projection front.

**$375.00 - 425.00**

COMMODE WASHSTAND—wooden top with splash back, burl trim on drawer and doors, machine lines.
**$325.00 - 375.00**

COMMODE WASHSTAND—wooden top with splash back, burl veneer banding on drawers and door, incised lines and carving.
**$325.00 - 375.00**

COMMODE WASHSTAND—wooden top with splash back, applied circular molding on drawer, applied ornaments chamfered corner stiles, molded door frames.
**$250.00 - 300.00**

COMMODE WASHSTAND—wooden top with high splash back and shelves, veneered door panels with molded frames, applied burl veneer panels on drawer, upper corner stile, and splash back, fluted corner stiles.
**$400.00 - 450.00**

**LIFT TOP COMMODE**—applied circular molding and ornaments door panels and chamfered corner stiles.

$325.00 - 350.00

**COMMODE WASHSTAND**—incised lines and carving, molded drawer with applied molding, applied carved molding on door, fluted corner stiles; (this piece was listed as a Somnoe and was priced at $27.00 in 1876.)

$275.00 - 300.00

**BUREAU WASHSTAND**—splash back, applied molding around drawers, applied ornaments on chamfered corner stiles, projection front.

**$350.00 - 375.00**

**BUREAU WASHSTAND**—splash back, towel rod, molded drawer panels, chamfered corner stiles.

$300.00 - 350.00

BUREAU WASHSTAND—splash back, towel rod, applied circular drawer molding, applied ornaments on chamfered corner stiles.   **$375.00 - 400.00**

BUREAU WASHSTAND—splash back, applied panels on drawers, applied carved molding on corner stiles, projection front.   **$275.00 - 325.00**

BUREAU WASHSTAND—splash back, applied molded panels on drawers, applied ornaments on chamfered corner stiles.   **$275.00 - 325.00**

BUREAU WASHSTAND—splash back, applied panels on drawers and corner stiles, incised lines.   **$250.00 - 300.00**

111

BUREAU WASHSTAND—splash back, molded drawer panels, rounded corner stiles.

$275.00 - 300.00

BUREAU WASHSTAND—molded drawers, applied ornaments on chamfered corner stiles, projection front.

$275.00 - 325.00

BUREAU WASHSTAND—machine lines and carving on drawers and corner stiles.

$275.00 - 300.00

BUREAU WASHSTAND—low splash back, brass escutcheons, plank ends, plain front, depth only 13½".

$250.00 - 300.00

BUREAU WASHSTAND—beveled drawer edges, rounded corner stiles, plain front.

$250.00 - 300.00

BUREAU WASHSTAND—splash back, towel bars, plain front.

$300.00 - 350.00

BUREAU WASHSTAND—splash back chamfered corner stiles with applied ornaments, plain front, poplar wood stained walnut. $225.00 - 275.00

BUREAU WASHSTAND—marble top, applied circular molding, burl veneer drawer panels, applied carving around key holes, chamfered corner stiles with applied ornaments. $325.00 - 350.00

DRESSER—wooden top, swing mirror, 2 decks, molded drawers, applied ornaments.

$375.00 - 425.00

DRESSER—wooden top, swing mirror, 2 decks, incised lines, incised and paneled pediment, plain front.

$350.00 - 400.00

DRESSER—wooden top, swing mirror, 2 boxes, applied circular and ring molding on drawers, projection front, applied carving on corner stiles, fret work above mirror.

$475.00 - 525.00

DRESSER—wooden top, swing mirror, 2 boxes, applied circular and ring molding on drawers, projection front, applied carving on chamfered corner stiles, molded and paneled pediment.

$550.00 - 600.00

DRESSER—wooden top, 2 decks, applied circular molding on top drawer, projection front, applied ornaments on corner stiles.                    **$275.00 - 325.00**

DRESSER—wooden top, 2 decks, molded burl veneer panels on drawers and corner stiles, projection front, pilasters on corner stiles.                    **$275.00 - 325.00**

DRESSER—wooden top, wishbone mirror, 2 decks, crotch veneer on drawer fronts, projection front, fret work on top of mirror frame, applied ornaments on rounded corner stiles, serpentine front. **$550.00 - 600.00**

DRESSER—wooden top, wishbone mirror, 2 boxes, projection front, applied ornaments on chamfered corner stiles.                    **$350.00 - 400.00**

DRESSER—wooden top, wishbone mirror, 2 decks, molded burl veneer panels on drawers, fret work above mirror frame.
**$450.00 - 500.00**

DRESSER—wooden top, wishbone mirror, 2 decks, applied panels on drawers, projection front, applied ornaments on corner stiles.
**$375.00 - 425.00**

DRESSER—wooden top, applied molding around drawers, projections front, applied ornaments on chamfered corner stiles, composition pulls.
**$275.00 - 300.00**

DRESSER—wooden top, applied circular molding on drawers, applied ornaments on chamfered corner stiles.
**$350.00 - 400.00**

DRESSER—wooden top, molded burl veneer panels on drawers, veneer trim, incised lines and carving on chamfered corner stiles.

$325.00 - 350.00

DRESSER—wooden top, molded drawers, projection front, applied ornaments on corner stiles.

$200.00 - 250.00

DRESSING CASE—wooden top, mirror set in frame, applied burl veneer panels on drawers, corner stiles and mirror frame, incised lines and carving on pediment.

$375.00 - 425.00

DRESSER—marble top, swing mirror, 2 boxes, applied circular and ring molding on drawers, applied carving on corner stiles, molded and paneled pediment.

**$600.00 - 650.00**

DRESSER—marble top, projection front, applied circular and ring molding on drawers, applied carving on rounded corner stiles. **$400.00 - 450.00**

DRESSER—marble top, applied burl veneer panels on drawers, fluted corner stiles.

**$350.00 - 400.00**

DRESSER—marble top, swing mirror, 2 boxes, applied circular molding on drawers, fret work around mirror frame. **$600.00 - 650.00**

DRESSER—marble top, mirror set in frame, center deck, applied ring molding and molded veneer panels on drawers, projection front, incised lines and applied carving on corner stiles, molded and paneled pediment.

**$800.00 - 850.00**

DRESSER—marble insert, swing mirror, 2 decks, applied burl veneer panels on drawers and mirror frame, incised and paneled pediment.    $350.00 - 400.00

DRESSER—marble insert, 2 decks, molded burl veneer panels on drawers and corner stiles.

$250.00 - 300.00

DRESSING CASE—marble top, applied burl veneer panels on drawers, mirror frame and corner stiles, original pediment and shelves missing.    $250.00 - 300.00

DRESSING CASE—marble top, applied burl veneer panels on drawers and mirror frame, molded and paneled pediment.    $450.00 - 500.00

DRESSING CASE—marble top, applied burl veneer panels on drawers, corner stiles and mirror frame, applied ornaments, applied molding around lower drawers.
$500.00 - 550.00

CHIFFONIER—machine lines and carving, corner stile contains locking device for all drawers.
$400.00 - 450.00

DRESSING CASE—marble top, applied molding around drawers, applied burl veneer panels on drawers, applied carving on corner stiles, and mirror frame, molded pediment.
$500.00 - 550.00

BEDSTEAD—7' 3", crotch veneer panels, applied carving and burl veneer panels, machine lines and carving.

COMMODE WASHSTAND—marble top with high splash back and corner soap shelves, burl veneer banding on drawers and door, applied panels, machine lines and carving.

DRESSER—7' 3", marble top, veneer banding on drawers, applied carving and burl veneer panels, machine lines and carving. (Eastlake)

**3 Piece Set:   $2,500.00 - 2,750.00**

BEDSTEAD—8′ 7″, rich crotch veneer panels, applied veneer panels, applied molding, carving and ornaments, molded and paneled pediment.

DRESSING CASE—8′ 9″, rich crotch veneer drawer fronts, applied veneer panels, applied molding, carving and ornaments, molded and paneled pediment.

**2 Piece Set:   $3,000.00 - 3,500.00**  (Renaissance Revival)

WARDROBE—7′ 4″, tall, 3′ 4″ wide, molded door frames, applied panels on dresser, molded base.
$400.00 - 450.00

WARDROBE—6′ 6″ tall, 3′ 8″ wide plain front, applied ornaments.
$300.00 - 350.00

122

WARDROBE—8′ tall, 4′ wide, applied circular molding, molded door frames, applied pediment with rosette and panels. $750.00 - 900.00

WARDROBE—8′ 9″ tall, 5′ wide, crotch veneer door panels, applied molding on drawers and door, applied carved panels and carved ornaments, molded pediment with carved crest. **$1,500.00 - 1,600.00**

*SINGLE BEDSTEAD—4′ 8″ tall, applied ornaments, molded foot rail and molded head rail surmounted by molded carved crest. **$300.00 - 350.00**

*BEDSTEAD—5′ 8″ tall, molded foot rail with applied molding, headboard decorated with burl veneer, applied panels and molded crest. **$450.00 - 550.00**

*(1876 PRICES—$7.00 - 13.00)

SPOOL BEDSTEAD WITH LOW POSTS—triangular shaped headboard surmounted by applied spool ornaments.
$375.00 - 400.00

ROPE BEDSTEAD WITH SPOOL TURNINGS—high posts, headboard surmounted with applied spool ornaments.
$500.00 - 600.00

*BEDSTEAD—7' 2" tall, applied burl veneer panel on footboard; headboard decorated with recessed burl veneer panel, burl veneer applied panels, applied moldings and ornaments, molded and paneled pediment.
$800.00 - 900.00

*BEDSTEAD—7' tall, molded foot rail with applied molding, applied molding and carved ornament on footboard, headboard decorated with urn finials, applied molding and ornaments with heavily pierced and carved pediment.
$1,000.00 - 1,200.00

*(1876 PRICES—$19.00 - 57.00)

124

"JENNY LIND" SPOOL BEDSTEAD.

$275.00 - 325.00

*BEDSTEAD—7′ 6″ tall, machine lines and carving, burl veneer centered panels, carved and pierced pediment. (Eastlake)

**$1,000.00 - 1,100.00**

*BEDSTEAD—8′ tall, recessed veneer panels surrounded by molded frame, applied incised panels, applied carved ornament, urn finials, top rail with applied molding, heavy carved and pierced pediment.

**$1,000.00 - 1,200.00**

HALF TESTER BEDSTEAD—7′ tall, molded headboard panels, turned headboard posts.

$1250.00 - 1500.00

*(1876 PRICES—$19.00 - 100.00)

125

DRESSING MIRROR—23½" high, 20½" wide, mahogany veneer. (Empire transitional)

$150.00 - 175.00

TOWEL ROD—single end uprights with 3 horizontal rods.

$80.00 - 100.00

WALL MOUNTED GROOMING MIRROR—21" high, 11½" wide.

$125.00 - 150.00

*TRESTLE TOWEL RACK—molded top with 5 horizontal rods.

$100.00 - 125.00

*(1876 PRICES— 75c - $1.00)

126

*TRESTLE TOWEL RACK—arched and molded top with 5 horizontal rods.

$100.00 - 125.00

WALL MOUNTED TOWEL RACK—fret top, turned rods.

$125.00 - 150.00

# Chapter 8
## Sleep My Child

In some Victorian homes there was a special room for the baby and toddlers—the nursery. Here small furniture was desirable.

Baby bed frames, while much smaller, emulated the adult versions. High solid headboards were the norm for large ones so the wee sizes had them too. If the family preferred simplier country furniture, spool frames were available. The spindled sides which kept the infant from rolling out were an example of the lathe machine's work. Lengths varied from a petite crib with high spindles to the youth type which five-or six-year-olds might use. This latter had low sides which a child could easily crawl over getting in and out of bed. Yet they sufficed to keep a twisting, turning sleepy head from plunging off onto the floor. Cribs could be single or double, but cradles were reserved for one occupant.

Remember, "Rock-a-bye baby in the tree top" may be a nostalgic lullabye, but a much better way is to tuck the wee one in a comfortable cradle where he can be snug, safe, and sleepy without being endangered by a breaking bough. Cradles from eighteenth century America were often made with solid sides and a hood which sheltered the baby's head from drafts and light. Early settlers found pine in abundance and frequently used this soft wood to carve out a safe sleeping spot for their infants.

By the 1800's, cradles were more sophisticated, partly because homes could be heated by stoves instead of fireplaces so that cold drafts were less of a problem and partly because of the development of machines which replaced handwork in the construction process. Cradles with many spindles plus turned corner posts rocked gently on curved slats.

Some cradles with solid ends rested on a platform so that they could sway back and forth. A peg or lever permitted them to be locked into a stationary position. Some of these bear a late 1800's patent date. Other types were suspended on frames to move when their occupants stirred and functioned without the added aid of the wind blowing through a temperamental tree bough.

Occasionally one sees other articles of, as a child might say "just the size of me" furniture made for the junior generation of the past. For example, little rockers, designed to match the grown up ones, bring premium prices because they are rarer than the larger variety. A popular style has a cane back and seat and rectangular lines—a representative of the late Victorian period. Doll collectors especially enjoy finding child-size articles to help exhibit their toy children in natural ways. Some rock in cradles, sit in high chairs, recline in bed, sway in swings, or rock in rocking chairs. How would a collector demonstrate the use of a high back chair built close to the floor when said chair has a hole in the seat? Would a small chamber pot be inserted beneath the hole and a doll be placed on the seat as though she were being educated in bathroom manners? It would take a little ingenuity to display yesteryear's nursery necessity (known as a necessary chair) tastefully in public. Nursery essentials don't seem to change too much down through the years.

PLATFORM CRADLE WITH SPINDLES—21″ x 38½″,
41″ high.

$450.00 - 500.00

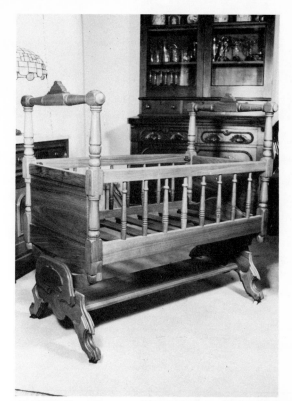

PLATFORM CRADLE WITH SPINDLED SIDES AND
SOLID ENDS—21″ x 38½″, 39″ high.

$450.00 - 500.00

PLATFORM CRADLE WITH SPINDLES—21″ x 38½″,
39″ high.

$375.00 - 425.00

*ROCKER CRADLE—spool turnings, 20″ x 37½″, 32″
high.

$300.00 - 350.00

*(1876 PRICE—$3.00)

*ROCKER CRADLE—slat decorations, 21″ x 38½″.

$200.00 - 225.00

—BABY BEDSTEAD—39″ x 57″, 37″ high, spindle sides, solid ends, applied ornament and finials on posts.

$300.00 - 350.00

*CRADLE ON WHEELS—(wheels have been added), 21″ x 39″, 33″ high, spool turnings.

$250.00 - 275.00

*(1876 PRICE—$3.00)

—BABY BEDSTEAD—37½″ x 50½″, 35″ high, solid headboard with applied molding and carving on head and foot board.

$300.00 - 350.00

—(1876 PRICE—$5.00)

130

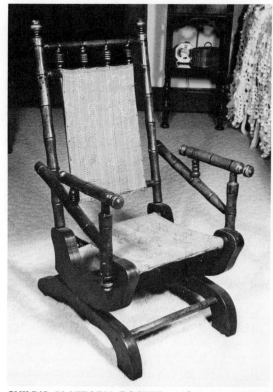

YOUTH BEDSTEAD—41″ x 64½″, 49½″ high, spindles at sides and end, solid headboard with molded panels, applied ornament, finials on posts.     **$450.00 - 500.00**

CHILD'S PLATFORM ROCKER—11″ to seat, 33½″ high.

**$200.00 - 225.00**

CHILD'S ROCKER—round caned seat, demi-arms, rectangular caned back, incised lines, 11″ to seat, 27″ high.     **$250.00 - 275.00**

CHILD'S NECESSARY CHAIR ON ROCKERS
**$125.00 - 150.00**

# Chapter 9
## Aunt Jessie's Attic

Did Victorian manufacturers and dealers consider it vulgar to state prices in their advertisments? It almost seems as if this were true when the stacks of one hundred year old newspapers and magazines up in "Aunt Jessie's attic" are examined. Wareroom operators boast about their excellent merchandise but forget figures. Thus it was difficult to secure original prices. Here are a few typical ads.

**The Spirit of the Age,** Madison, Indiana, June 29, 1874. C. Vail Undertaker has always on hand a large stock of latest style FURNITURE at the lowest prices.

Here's the exception to the rule: **Indianapolis Daily Sentinel,** April 16, 1874. See our chamber suits $30 & $1500 Mitchell & Rammelsberg Furniture Co.

**The Cincinnati Daily Enquirer,** Thursday Morning, July 29, 1875. A.C. Richards, Designer and Manufacturer of Plain, Medium, and Fine Furniture. Prices lower than any other house in the city. Special attention given to ordered work.

and

L.F. Wehrman & Son, Wholesale and Retail Furniture Warerooms Are Offering Special Inducements to Purchasers . . . a large assorted stock of Fine and Common Furniture . . . We invite you to call and see our Stock.

The November, 1886 **Art Amateur** magazine advertises ANTIQUES while Allard & Sons and Prignot boasts of French Furniture and Interior Decorations. Their work may be found in the New York dwellings of Cornelius Vanderbilt, Ogden Goelet, and Dr. Seward Webb.

In the same publication Charles Tisch, designer and maker of furniture "Asks attention to the new and beautiful examples of Fine Cabinet Furniture and Upholstery now on Exhibition at his Warerooms, which are offered at attractive prices." They are located "Fourth House from Messrs. Tiffany & Co."

**The Spirit of the Age,** Madison, Indiana, May 9, 1874, brings a furniture factory alive with the description of "Our Manufactories".

"We have this week gone through the furniture factory and finishing shops of H.F. Robbins & Co. We in childhood played about the old factory, & many a basket of shavings have we carried home. Home! how pleasant the thought and what sweet recollections it calls up. The hum of the machinery, the buzz of the planers, the smell of the shavings as they curled away from the turners, led us back to twenty years ago, but they have a great deal of new machinery unknown then. In all their different departments, they now work from 80 to 100 men, and turn out from 100 to 250 bedsteads per day, ranging in price from $3 to $100 each. All kinds and classes of furniture are manufactured at these shops, bureaus, extension tables, wardrobes, dressing cases, chamber suits, ranging in price from $20 to $200. They have about $125,000 invested in their business, and pay out about $50,000 per year for materials, etc. Their receipts average about $200,000 yearly.

"This factory commenced in 1852 and at that time was the only steam furniture manufactory, except one at Lawrenceburg in this State, or between Cincinnati and St. Louis. Their business extends from New York westwardly through the Middle, Western, and Southern States to Texas. Some idea of their extensive business can be had when we consider that they now have on hand about 4,000 bedsteads, besides other furniture. The factory is a two story brick, 50 by 110 feet, with frame building adjacent 35 by 50 feet. Store and finishing shop on Main X, 60 feet front, running back 168, besides a wareroom on West Street."

Times were changing rapidly, and **The Spirit of the Age** reporter knew it. The Industrial Revolution completely altered Victoria's world.

# Glossary

**Applied**
an ornamentation crafted separately and attached to a piece later. Applied cresting is attached to the top rail of a chair or sofa. Applied ornament is a detail added to the surface of a piece.

**Apron**
a piece used as a connecting "skirt" in chairs, cabinets, and tables. It may be a structural aid or it might hide the construction. The apron is found at the base of cabinets, cupboards, and chests: between the feet. In a table, it is beneath the top where the legs connect. In a chair, it is the portion under the seat.

**Arched Molding**
a half round convex strip used for trim.

**Armoire**
a big cupboard or wardrobe of the type which were used originally in the Middle Ages to store arms and armour.

**Bail handle**
a drawer pull with a brass half loop pendent fastened to a back plate.

**Balloon back**
a chair back which bears a vague resemblance to a round balloon.

**Banding**
a strip of inlay whose color contrasts with the surrounding wood or a narrow border of veneering on drawer fronts.

**Beading**
a thin strip of molding which resembles small beads linked together in a continuous line.

**Bevel**
a slanting edge cut on a board or sheet of glass.

**Breakfront**
a central vertical part projects out from the main structure to break the straight line between its top and base portion. Used on some bookcases, desks, sideboards, wardrobes.

**Broken pediment**
a top ornament which does not meet completely at the apex (highest point).

**Burl**
an abnormal growth on trees which can be sliced thin to make decorative veneers.

**Cabriole leg**
a leg which flows out at the knee and in at the ankle, then slightly outward again to make a double curve.

**Cane**
long narrow strip of rattan used for weaving chair seats and backs.

**Canopy**

the framework on top of the tall posts of a bed (resembles a roof over the bed). Also called a tester.

**Case piece**

the box like structure which forms the outside of a cabinet, desk, chest of drawers, or etc.

**Chamfer**

1.) an edge or corner cut off to make a slanting surface
2.) a groove cut in wood

**Cheval glass**

a large mirror which swings from vertical posts, sits on the floor, and reflects a full-length view or its small counterpart which sits on a table or chest and may include a drawer as well as the mirror. (cheval means horse in French, hence a support)

**Chip carving**

a simple carved ornament made with a chisel or gauge.

**Circular molding**

an ornamental strip applied or carved on furniture in a circular or oval contour. It may be incised or raised.

**Commode**

comes from the French word meaning convenient. A washstand with an enclosed cupboard.

**Composition**

a plaster of Paris, rosin, sizing and water mixture molded to resemble carving.

**Corner stile**

the upright at the corner of a piece of furniture.

**Cornice**

the top horizontal molding on some article of furniture.

**Crest**

a carved piece on the top rail of a sofa or chair.

**Cresting**

the ornamental top of a pediment, chair, settee, or sofa back.

**Crotch-grain veneer**

thin strips of wood cut from the place where the branch intersects with the trunk of the tree, used over base woods because of its decorative "V" shape.

**Cylinder**

a curved sliding top on a desk or secretary front or a desk or secretary which has such a front. A venetian-blind type is not usually considered a true cylinder which should be a solid piece.

**Cyma curve**

a half convex, half concave, continuous curve as seen in a cabriole leg.

**Davenport**

An illustration in an 1876 Grand Rapids furniture price list refers to a desk of this type as a lady's desk and does not mention a davenport. Others define it as a small writing desk used during the 1800's. The sloping top lifts up so that articles could be stored beneath, and usually, the drawers pull out sideways instead of in the front.

**Demi-arm**

and hip rest seem to be current terms to describe the partial arms on some chairs.

**Dowel**

a pin or peg which fits into holes in two pieces of wood to hold them together. Old pegs are apt to be square appearing.

**Drop front**

a hinged lid on a desk which drops down to form a writing surface.

**Eastlake**
Charles Lock Eastlake published a book in 1868 on household taste which blasted the over-ornamented, cheaply made furniture the machine age was producing. He wanted conscious design in furniture and emphasized straight lines and Gothic and Japanese ornamentation. However, manufacturers took his rectangular lines and overdecorated them. This produced an Eastlake style in furniture, circa 1870-1890.

**Ebony and gilt drops**
term found in 1800 catalogs for drawer pulls now called "tear drop". An almost pear-shaped black pendent is attached to a round brass plate.

**Eclectic**
Copying, using, and adapting the designs and styles of previous periods.

**Escutcheon**
a fitting around a keyhole. Often made of brass or wood; it may be inset or applied.

**Etagère**
overly large and fancy whatnot with a mirror and shelves for displaying bric-a-brac.

**Extension table**
the table top splits open so that additional leaves may be inserted to enlarge it.

**Fall front**
a hinged flap on a desk which drops open to form a writing surface.

**Fielding panel**
a panel with the main surface framed by molding, beveling, or grooving.

**Finger grip**
a groove cut in the lower edge of a drawer front to use in place of a handle or knob.

**Finger Roll**
continuous concave molding cut into the frame of a chair or sofa.

**Finial**
a turned, carved, or cast end ornament on a clock, table, bedstead post, or pediment.

**Flush**
level with the surrounding surface.

**Fret or Fretwork**
an ornamental border, perforated or cut in low relief, perhaps in geometric patterns.

**Gallery**
a raised railing or rim of wood or metal around a desk, table, sideboard, or etc.

**Gateleg**
a swinging leg with a stretcher that serves as a support for a table leaf.

**Geometric**
a pattern made by interlacing circles, triangles, squares, and similar designs.

**Hip rest**
appears to be a modern term for a partial arm on chairs, sometimes called demi-arm currently.

**Incise**
design cut into or engraved in the surface.

**Inlay**
forming designs by inserting contrasting colors, grains, and textures flush in wood using wood, metal, shells, or ivory.

**Inset pilaster**
an artificial, decorative pillar inserted in a flat surface, most frequently at the front corners of a case piece.

**Laminated**
layers of wood glued together with the grain of each succeeding layer at right angles to the ones adjacent. Makes a strong surface.

**Louis XV**
French style that emulated Louis XV (reigned 1715-1774). Graceful curves and elliptical shapes. Dainty. Cabriole leg. Floral carvings.

**Molding**
a continuous ornamental edging applied to or carved in furniture.

**Ogee**
a molding with a double continuous curve.

**Panel**
a square or rectangular board held in place by a grooved framework. A sunken panel is beneath the framework, and a flush one has the same height as the frame and is usually molded. A raised panel rises slightly above the surrounding surface, and it is often molded.

**Pediment**
an ornamental top on a piece of furniture.

**Pendent finial**
a downward finial. (A finial is a turned, carved, or cast terminal ornament.)

**Pie crust**
decorative edge on a table which resembles the way a housewife crimps the edge of a pie crust.

**Pier glass or mirror**
a tall narrow mirror often hung between two long windows.

**Pierced carving**
open work carving.

**Pilaster**
a decorative artificial pillar with no structural strength set against a background. Often it is half round or rectangular.

**Projection front**
A top that sticks out over the rest of the piece. A projecting top drawer overhangs the other drawers.

**Pull brackets**
the slides located one on either side of a desk or secretary which pull out to support the pulled down writing flap.

**Pull slides**
See definition above.

**Raised panel**
a panel which projects slightly above the surrounding surface and is often molded.

**Renaissance**
Revival of interest in ancient Greek and Roman culture. Elaborate carving. Heavy, imposing, ornamented furniture. Circa 1850-1885.

**Ring molding**
a circular ornamental edging applied to or carved in furniture.

**Rococo**
derived from two French words meaning rock and shell. Elaborate decorations with rocks, shells, and other natural objects such as fruits and flowers.

**Rounded end**
the curved rather than straight end of case pieces. An 1870's price list speaks of "round corners".

**Rung**
the simple or decorative cross piece which connects cabinet, chair, or table legs at the bottom. A runner.

**Runner**
1.) another name for the rocker on a rocking chair.
2.) a guide strip to support a drawer.
3.) slides on which the drop fronts on desks are supported.

**Scalloped**
(A Grand Rapid's 1870's price list spells this word with two p's.) a series of curves forming an ornamental edge derived from a shell shape (scallop).

**Serpentine**
a wavy, snake-like curve that is convex at the center and ends and concave between.

**Skirt**
(apron) often used as a decorative means to hide the construction of a piece, for example, where the legs are attached to the top of a table. Found near the base of cabinets or chests and beneath the seat on chairs.

**Slant front**
the hinged fall lid on a desk or secretary which provides a writing surface when dropped open and slants back when closed.

**Slat**
1.) horizontal crossbars in chair backs.
2.) flat wooden pieces which fit between the rails of a bed to support the springs.
3.) Sometimes a rocker on a rocking chair is called a curved slat.

**Slip seat**
an upholstered seat which is removable.

**Splat**
the plain or ornamental center upright in a chair back.

**Spool turning**
resembles spools, knobs, balls, or like objects strung together in a row.

**Spoon back**
a chair back curved to fit the contour of the human body.

**Stile**
the vertical piece in a frame or panel in furniture.

**Stretchers**
the rungs or crosspieces which connect cabinet, table, or chair legs.

**Teapoy**
small table for tea service.

**Tester**
the roof like framework on top of the tall posts of a bed. A half-tester would cover the head of the bed only. (canopy)

**Tilt-top**
a table top hinged to its base so it can be tipped to a vertical position.

**Tripod table**
table with a pedestal supported by three out-curved legs.

**Turning**
shaping wood on a lathe with chisels.

**Urn**
a decorative vase with a base used as a finial on furniture.

**Veneer**
a thin layer of decorative wood glued over the surface of a cheaper wood.

**Victorian Era**
the years covered by the reign of Queen Victoria in England, 1837-1901.

**Whatnot**
a tier of shelves connected by turned posts used to display knickknacks.

# Bibliography

1. Aronson, Joseph, **Encyclopedia of Furniture**, New York, N.Y., Crown Publishers, Inc., 1965.

2. Bradford, Ernle, **Dictionary of Antiques**, London, England, The English Universities Press Ltd., 1963.

3. Century Furniture Company, **Furniture as Interpreted by the Century Furniture Company**, Grand Rapids, Michigan, 1926.

4. Grand Rapids Furniture Festival Souvenir Program, **Romance of Furniture**, Grand Rapids, Michigan, July 8, 9, 10, 1936.

5. Grotz, George, **The New Antiques**, Garden City, N.Y., Doubleday & Company, 1964.

6. Nelson, Matter & Co., Catalog, **Manufacturers of Furniture**, Grand Rapids, Michigan, January 1st, 1873.

7. Nelson, Matter & Co., Catalog, **Manufacturers of Furniture**, Grand Rapids, Michigan, March, 1876.

8. Nesbit, Wilbur D., **The Story of Berkey & Gay**, Reprinted, with slight additions, from **Musey's Magazine** of September, 1911.

9. Norbury, James, **The World of Victoriana**, London, England, Hamlyn, 1972.

10. Ormsbee, Thomas H., **Field Guide to American Victorian Furniture**, Boston, Mass., Little, Brown and Company, 1952.

11. Ransom, Frank Edward, **The City Built on Wood, a History of the Furniture Industry in Grand Rapids, Michigan**, Ann Arbor, Michigan, Edwards Bros., Inc., 1955.

12. Shull, Thelma, **Victorian Antiques**, Rutland, Vermont, Charles E. Tuttle Company, 1963.

13. Symonds, R.W., and Whineray, B.B., **Victorian Furniture**, London, Country Life Limited, 1962.

14. Winchester, Alice, **How To Know American Antiques**, The New American Library, New York, N.Y., 1951.

plus various late 1800's periodicals scrounged from "Aunt Jessie's Attic".

# AFRICA IS NOT A COUNTRY

## 2ND EDITION

MARGY BURNS KNIGHT

MARK MELNICOVE

ILLUSTRATED BY ANNE SIBLEY O'BRIEN

**M** Millbrook Press • Minneapolis

Tunis

Algiers

**TUNISIA**

Rabat

ATLAS MOUNTAINS

**MOROCCO**

Tripoli

Laâyoune

**WESTERN SAHARA**

**ALGERIA**

**LIBYA**

AHAGGAR MOUNTAINS

Cairo

**EGYPT**

RED SEA

NILE RIVER

S A H A R A   D E S E R T

TIBESTI MOUNTAINS

**MAURITANIA**

Nouakchott

**MALI**

**NIGER**

Khartoum

**ERITREA**

Asmara

**CABO
VERDE**

SENEGAL RIVER

Praia

**SENEGAL**

Dakar

Bamako

Niamey

**CHAD**

BLUE NILE

**SUDAN**

**GAMBIA**

Banjul

Ouagadougou

**GUINEA-BISSAU**

Bissau

**BURKINA
FASO**

N'Djamena

**DJIBOUTI**

Djibouti

SIGER RIVER

**GUINEA**

**NIGERIA**

THE HORN
OF AFRICA

Conakry

**CÔTE
D'IVOIRE**

Abuja

**SOUTH SUDAN**

Freetown

**SIERRA LEONE**

Yamoussoukro

**CENTRAL AFRICAN
REPUBLIC**

Addis Ababa

Monrovia

**LIBERIA**

Juba

**ETHIOPIA**

WHITE NILE

**CAMEROON**

Bangui

**SOMALIA**

Malabo

Yaoundé

**DEMOCRATIC
REPUBLIC
OF THE CONGO**

**UGANDA**

**KENYA**

**EQUATORIAL GUINEA**

Libreville

São Tomé

Kampala

Mogadishu

**SÃO TOMÉ
& PRÍNCIPE**

**GABON**

CONGO RIVER

**RWANDA**

Kigali

Lake
Victoria

Nairobi

**SEYCHELLES**

Brazzaville

Gitega

MOUNT KILIMANJARO

Victoria

Kinshasa

**BURUNDI**

**TANZANIA**

Luanda

Dodoma

**COMOROS**

Moroni

**ANGOLA**

**MADAGASCAR**

Lilongwe

**ZAMBIA**

Lusaka

ZAMBEZI RIVER

Antananarivo

Harare

Port Louis

**NAMIBIA**

**ZIMBABWE**

**MOZAMBIQUE**

**MAURITIUS**

**BOTSWANA**

LIMPOPO RIVER

Windhoek

Gaborone

Pretoria

Maputo

Kalahari
Desert

Mbabane

**ESWATINI**

ORANGE RIVER

DRAKENSBERG MOUNTAINS

Maseru

**LESOTHO**

**SOUTH
AFRICA**

Accra

**GHANA**

**TOGO**

Lomé

**BENIN**

Porto Novo

**REPUBLIC OF THE CONGO**

Desert

Grasslands

Tropical rain forest

2

*Africa is not a country—it is a vast continent made up of fifty-four nations. If you took the land of the United States and added it to the lands of China, Japan, and Europe, Africa would still be bigger.*

*From the tiny island nations of Comoros, Seychelles, and São Tomé and Príncipe, to its largest country (Algeria), Africa is the only continent with land in all four hemispheres. Unlike any other continent, it is divided into two almost equal lengths by the equator, and it is nearly as wide as it is long.*

*If you drew a picture of Africa's landscapes on a large pie and cut it into ten equal pieces, only one piece would contain all of its rain forests. Four pieces would represent the deserts; another four would be mostly grass, farmland, and trees. The final piece would hold all the mountains and cities of this beautiful, vibrant continent, where several hundred million children wake up every morning.*

The sun is just rising as Arim and Efrem get up to prepare for school. They take showers, change into school uniforms, and comb their hair while listening to children's programs on the radio. After a breakfast of sweet, hot tea and bread with butter and marmalade, they put on their book bags.

Their parents gently place their hands on their heads and say, "May God be with you the whole day." The boys kiss their parents' hands and respond "*Yekenielai*," which means "thank you" in Tigrinya, a widely spoken language in ERITREA. Before they walk out of the door with their father, who is going to his office in downtown Asmara, the boys are reminded by their mother to always respect their teachers and elders.

It is early morning in Palepo, a village in CAMEROON. Before breakfast, Mantoh spends an hour selling fresh milk from the gourd she carries on her head. Tepe washes the dishes while Nkolo and Folla collect firewood and take several trips to the well. Their chores will be complete when there is enough water and firewood for the day. After a breakfast of *pap*, a cereal made from corn, the children will walk to school with their friends.

Classes start in a few minutes. Kip and Arangi know they won't be late because they are so quick. Every day they run several miles to school through the highlands of KENYA. Both Arangi and Kip want to join a running team when they get to high school. They love to run long distances. When they are older, the children hope to train as marathon runners, so that they can compete with the fastest racers from all over the world.

With *pula* in hand, Mapula walks to a corner store to buy fresh bread for breakfast. *Pula* is the name of the currency in BOTSWANA; it is also the word for rain in Setswana, a language spoken by over four million people. Since rain is often scarce, it is very important to the people who live there. Sometimes babies are named after the different kinds of rain. Mapula is a name for "mother of rain."

On wintry July mornings, Thomas and his father wrap blankets around their shoulders to keep warm in the Drakensberg Mountains of LESOTHO. *Lehloa* is a word for snow in Sesotho, the main language spoken in Lesotho. There are very few words for snow in Africa's two thousand other languages, because it never snows in most countries. In Lesotho the paths can be slippery, so father and son use mountain-savvy ponies to travel to the market, and then to visit friends and relatives.

9

Mona, Basma, and Hala spill out of their homes in Cairo to walk to school on jammed sidewalks. Mona likes to leave early so that she can stop at the kiosk to buy hot, spicy beans and bread for breakfast. The students walk by early morning traffic jams, passing apartment buildings and ancient mosques. If they choose to walk down by the Nile, they would see ships from all over the world anchored in the river's harbors. Cairo, which means "victorious" in Arabic, is EGYPT's capital and one of Africa's largest cities.

11

As the teacher talks about their country's history, Abena and Doreen remember the dance they performed at last year's Independence Day parade. On March 6, 1957, the Gold Coast declared its independence from Britain and changed its name to GHANA. It was the first West African colony to become a nation. Today children in every African country celebrate an independence or nation day.

Chip, Farai, Rudo, and the other children are practicing for a choir concert later today in another part of Harare. They will sing two songs: one about the seasonal rains that help the crops to grow and the other about the abundance of wildlife in ZIMBABWE.

Each song will be sung in English and Shona. Zimbabwe means "stone enclosure" in Shona, which is both the name and language of the people who built the kingdom of Great Zimbabwe about seven hundred years ago.

Since before recorded history, children have enjoyed combining music, dance, and poetry in their play. Young girls in RWANDA keep this legacy alive by playing hand-clapping games such as *mabigibigi* in city neighborhoods as well as in rural communities. During recess in a schoolyard in Kigali, the country's capital, Bibiche, Rebero, and Nancy rhyme words, repeat phrases, carry melodies, and move their bodies in unison to the beats as they sing songs they've memorized. For generation after generation, girls have also improvised lyrics and passed them on from friend to friend, cousin to cousin, and sister to sister. While words change, the hand clapping, feet stomping, and joyous laughter continue to strengthen bonds that can last into adulthood.

Muhammed, Safi, and her baby sister do not stand too close to the tired camels, which have just finished a 500-mile (805 km) trek from the salt mines of northern MALI to Timbuktu. Founded upon an oasis, this nine-hundred-year-old city has long been associated with mystery and wealth. The valuable slabs of shiny, white salt, about 70 pounds (32 kg) each, will be taken off the camels and piled into taxis, which will drive the salt to boats bound for the city of Mopti on the Niger River. From Mopti, the salt will be loaded onto trucks headed for neighboring countries, whose peoples will use it to season their food.

On Fogo, an island within the island nation of CABO VERDE, Maria, Carolina, and Celso work in the fields. They have milked the goats and weeded the plants. Carolina shoos away the crows and keeps the hungry goats out of the watermelon and squash patches. Just before lunch the children dig up sweet potatoes. They will bring them to their father, José, who has been farming with them all morning. He will roast the potatoes over an open fire and serve them with goat's milk. All morning Lydia, his wife, has been selling goods to her customers in town. She will come home in time to eat lunch with her family before returning to her shop.

Every afternoon, sounds of kicking, passing, and scoring echo
through the backyards, streets, and parks of the coastal city of
Abidjan, in Côte d'Ivoire. Henri and his friends play soccer for hours
on end. In their neighborhood, all the players pitch in a few francs
to buy a ball. This time, Henri is "keeper of the ball." He will take it
home between games.

When not playing, the boys may be watching their favorite team on
television. If soccer games are not carried on TV, they are broadcast in
ten local languages on the radio.

In her family's tent in the Sahara desert in MAURITANIA, Fatima greets
afternoon guests with tea. As she pours the hot, sweet drink, her
sister, Asha, watches it foam in the glasses. While the grown-ups visit,
Fatima will paint Asha's hands with bright, intricate patterns made
from the powder of henna leaves.

Later, Fatima and Asha will share a *loha*, a wooden tablet used to
study verses from the Koran, the holy book of the Muslim people.
The girls will learn passages by chanting them out loud.

Priscilla and Mary have been traveling for several hours, so they are hungry. They poke their heads out of the window to buy some bananas, of which there are at least twenty varieties in TANZANIA. Today the girls have two choices.

Their uncle has gone into the *duka* to buy them cold drinks.
The girls hope that the man who drives the *basi* will soon tell all
of the passengers to get back on board. They want to get to their
grandmother's in time to play with their cousins before supper.

Every afternoon, Mariam, Oumar, and their friends play leapfrog and marbles on the beach in SENEGAL as they wait for the fishing boats to return with the day's catch. As soon as the boats are beached, the fishermen begin to divide the several hundred ocean perch and red fish. A few fish are given to those who helped to push the boats out into the surf that morning. Each fishing family gets a share of the fish. Even if a fisherman is sick and can't work, fish are set aside for his family. The remainder are often sold to a buyer from Dakar, who shows up in a truck.

Deehab and Makonne want their mother to hurry into the car so that they can get to the National Museum in Addis Ababa to see the "Lucy" exhibit. Lucy is one of the reasons that Africa is referred to as the Cradle of Humankind. More than three million years old, Lucy's remains were unearthed in 1974 in eastern ETHIOPIA. Paleoanthropologists were thrilled at how much of Lucy's skeleton was found. Only 40 inches (1 m) tall, Lucy was a full-grown hominid, and like us she walked on two legs. It is not known exactly how Lucy is related to modern-day humans. That is why it is exciting whenever a fossil is found in Africa— it may provide a missing link to our past.

Tadj and Josephine dig small holes in the sand of the REPUBLIC OF THE SUDAN to play a game of *siega*. Both children count and toss stones from hole to hole. Josephine wins because she captures the most stones. Almost immediately, Tadj sets up his stones for a second game.

*Siega*, which is called *gebeta* in Eritrea, *tsoro* in Zimbabwe, and *mancala* in Liberia, is played by children and grown-ups throughout Africa and the world. Many archaeologists think that *mancala* is one of the world's oldest games. Stone carvings of *mancala* boards have been found in ancient Egyptian pyramids and temples.

Ondel and Mbo have just finished soccer practice. Even though they are hungry, it is not time for supper. Hot and thirsty, they have plopped down on the couch, sipping from glasses of cool water as they watch cartoons. After the shows, the boys and Ondel's sister will go to Mbo's house to eat salted fish with mushrooms, *fufu*, and cassava leaves. If they are still hungry, they may go back to Ondel's house for more *fufu* and fish.

*Fufu* is made from cassava roots, which have been ground into flour and cooked in boiling water. These roots are bigger than a potato. The large, leafy greens of the cassava plant are a delicious vegetable enjoyed not only throughout the children's country, the DEMOCRATIC REPUBLIC OF THE CONGO, but elsewhere in tropical Africa.

28

Thandi and Thato are just home from school in Soweto, SOUTH AFRICA. They stayed after to practice a play about three Nobel Peace Prize winners from South Africa. Chief Albert John Luthuli, Archbishop Desmond Tutu, and President Nelson Mandela dedicated their lives to seeing that all people were treated fairly, regardless of their skin color.

   Their grandmother, Nombini, is home from work. She has cooked a large pot of curried chicken and vegetables. The children's mother, Mathabo, and their uncle Oliver will not return from their jobs in Johannesburg until after Thandi and Thato have washed the dishes and finished their homework.

The alluring fragrance of onions, red pepper, and ginger wafts through Ahmed's apartment in Algiers, the capital of ALGERIA. Tonight his mother has steamed and served couscous—the national dish—with spices and lamb in a big pan. Couscous, which is made from wheat, is sometimes mixed with honey, cinnamon, and almonds to make a dessert pudding. As the common plate of food is shared and savored, Ahmed and his family tell jokes and sip apricot juice.

Chuba wants to get it right. His father, uncles, and grandfathers are watching to see if he is dancing exactly the same way as they did when they were boys. Nearly every evening after supper, Chuba puts on his traditional outfit to practice the ancient dances of the Igbo of southeastern NIGERIA. As he concentrates on what his teachers are showing him, he wonders if he will be one of the few boys his age to be chosen to perform this year at weddings, Christmas celebrations, and harvest festivals. Other boys will be picked to sing and drum.

Aurala tells the first riddle because she yelled, "*Googga*"—"I am telling you a riddle," in Somali—before the others. They are playing *Googaalaysi*, a one-thousand-year-old game from SOMALIA.

"You are in a canoe and must cross the river with only three things: a goat, a cheetah, and a patch of grass. You can take only two items with you in the canoe at one time. You cannot take the goat with the grass or the cheetah with the goat, because the goat would eat the grass and the cheetah would eat the goat. So what do you do?"

With a huge grin, Samater shouts, "*Adale*"—"I know the answer."

"First, cross with the goat. Come back for the grass, drop it off, but after dropping it off, bring back the goat. Get the cheetah, but leave the goat behind. Finally, come back for the goat and cross the river."

Hodan cries, "*Googga*," and the game begins again.

It is just about dark when city bus number 15 from Antananarivo pulls up in front of the Tsimbazaza Zoo. Didier, Charlotte, and Benoit are the first three students to scramble off the bus. They quickly get in line to buy tickets for the night visit to watch the aye-aye, a nocturnal lemur that has ears like a bat and a tail like a fox. There are more than fifty lemur species in MADAGASCAR. The children are delighted to find that the tiny aye-aye are awake when they reach them.

The sun has set, the children have finished their chores and brushed their teeth, and the stars are shining in the sky over TOGO. Abla hopes to hear the story about market day held each Tuesday near her house. Afi wants to hear about the little girl and the lion. Koffi smiles as his father begins to speak.

"Once there was a wise little girl whose mother told her that if she was home alone, she should not let anyone in unless she heard the secret password." Though she has heard the story many times before, Afi's eyes grow wide when a sneaky lion tries to trick the girl into opening the door. But the lion doesn't know the password, and the girl is not fooled.

The children want another story, but it is late and they have to get up early for school. Before being tucked into bed, they will say prayers with their parents to give thanks for another long, full day.

ALGERIA (al-JIR-ee-uh)
Capital: Algiers (al-JIRZ). Population: 43.6 million.
Independence Day: July 5, 1962. Currency: Algerian dinar.

Soccer teams from Tunisia, Algeria, Nigeria, Cameroon, and South Africa competed with the best men's teams from around the globe at the 1998 World Cup in France. In the championship game, two of France's victorious goals against Brazil were scored by Zinedine Zidane, a French citizen, whose family is from Algeria.

ANGOLA (an-GOH-luh)
Capital: Luanda (loo-AHN-dah). Population: 33.6 million.
Independence Day: November 11, 1975. Currency: kwanza.

Angola's national dish, *Muamba de Galinha*, is a chicken stew that includes palm oil, tomatoes, okra, and squash. It is served with *funge*, a traditional side dish made from cassava flour.

BENIN (beh-NEEN)
Capital: Porto-Novo (PAWR-toh NOH-voh). Population: 13.3 million. Independence Day: August 1, 1960. Currency: West African CFA franc.

From the sixteenth to the late nineteenth century, Benin was known as the kingdom of Dahomey. Abomey was the capital of this wealthy state, which stretched into present-day Togo and Nigeria. Its ancient stories are woven into colorful tapestries by local artists and sold all over the world.

BOTSWANA (bots-WAH-nah)
Capital: Gaborone (gah-boh-ROH-nay). Population: 2.3 million. Independence Day: September 30, 1966. Currency: pula.

One hundred thebe equal 1 pula, and 11 pula equal about 1 US dollar. In addition to being the nation's currency, pula (meaning "rain") is also the national motto. The blue stripes on the flag represent rainwater.

BURKINA FASO (boor-KEE-nah FAH-soh)
Capital: Ouagadougou (wah-gah-DOO-goo). Population: 21.3 million. Independence Day: August 5, 1960. Currency: West African CFA franc.

Until 1984, Burkina Faso was called Upper Volta, after the headwaters of the Volta Rivers. Burkina Faso is a Mossi phrase that means "land of honorable people."

BURUNDI (boo-RUN-dee)
Capital: Gitega (gee-TAY-guh) (political capital), Bujumbura (boo-jum-BOO-rah) (commercial capital). Population: 12.2 million. Independence Day: July 1, 1962. Currency: Burundi franc.

Burundi lies two degrees below the equator in the Great Rift Valley. This series of deep cracks in Earth forms steep-sided valleys, which in Africa extend more than 3,000 miles (4,828 km) from Eritrea to Mozambique. The Great Rift Valley is known for its lakes, mountains, fertile soils, and fossils.

CABO VERDE (KAW-boh VAIR-day)
Capital: Praia (PRAH-yah). Population: 589,451.
Independence Day: July 5, 1975. Currency: escudo.

Cabo Verde is an archipelago of fifteen islands, 620 miles (998 km) off the coast of Senegal. Though known as the Green Cape, the islands can suffer long periods of drought. This is one reason why almost twice as many Cabo Verdeans live away from the islands as on them.

CAMEROON
Capital: Yaoundé (YAI-oun-DAI). Population: 28.5 million. Independence Day: January 1, 1960 (East Cameroon); October 1, 1961 (West Cameroon independence and federation with East Cameroon). Currency: Central African CFA franc.

Cameroonian children and their families usually share a taxi and the fare with strangers. This is called *taxi en ramassage*. *Ramassage* is a French word for "pickup."

CENTRAL AFRICAN REPUBLIC
Capital: Bangui (bahn-GEE). Population 5.3 million.
Independence Day: August 13, 1960. Currency: Central African CFA franc.

The Central African Republic is one of fourteen countries in Africa to use the CFA franc. Six countries use the Central African CFA franc and eight countries use the West African CFA franc. Even though they are two currencies, they work alike and are both linked to the exchange rate of the euro. The Economic Community of West African States has proposed a new currency called the eco that may eventually replace the CFA franc, which has been in circulation since 1945.

CHAD
Capital: N'Djamena (uhn-jah-MEE-nah). Population: 17.4 million. Independence Day: August 11, 1960. Currency: Central African CFA franc.

Chad's northern sector is in the Sahara, the world's largest desert. Sahara means "desert" in Arabic; it is about the same size as the continental United States. In addition to Chad, the Sahara stretches through Egypt, Tunisia, Libya, Sudan, Niger, Mauritania, Morocco, and Mali.

COMOROS (kah-MO-roz)
Capital: Moroni (mo-RO-nee). Population: 864,000.
Independence Day: July 6, 1975. Currency: Comorian franc.

Early Arab traders called Comoros "Islands of the Moon."
A crescent moon and stars appear on its stamps and flag. The
white crescent on the flag represents Islam, the country's
dominant religion.

CONGO (Democratic Republic of the Congo)
Capital: Kinshasa (KEEN-shah-suh). Population: 105 million.
Independence Day: June 30, 1960. Currency: Congolese franc.

The Ituri Forest is about the size of West Virginia. It is
home to the okapi, a hoofed mammal most closely related
to the giraffe, marked by black and white stripes on
its hindquarters.

CONGO (Republic of the Congo)
Capital: Brazzaville (BRAH-zuh-vil). Population: 5.4 million.

Independence Day: August 15, 1960.
Currency: Central African CFA franc.

Africa's second-longest river, the Congo,
flows for 2,900 miles (4,700 km), taking
the form of a huge counterclockwise arc,
mostly through the Democratic Republic of
the Congo. It forms a partial border with
the Republic of the Congo. It ranges in
width from 0.5 to 10 miles (0.8 to 16 km).
More than four thousand islands are located
in the river.

CÔTE D'IVOIRE (coat-dee-VWAHR)
Capital: Yamoussoukro (yah-moo-SOO-kro). Population:
28 million. Independence Day: August 7, 1960. Currency:
West African CFA franc.

The Basilique Notre-Dame de la Paix, "Our Lady of Peace,"
a near replica of St. Peter's in Rome, is the world's largest
church. In September 1990, Pope John Paul II traveled to
Yamoussoukro to dedicate the new basilica, which remains
controversial due to its expense and because so many
Muslims live in Côte d'Ivoire.

DJIBOUTI (ji-BOO-tee)
Capital: Djibouti. Population: 938,000. Independence Day:
June 27, 1977. Currency: Djiboutian franc.

Two of the colors on the Djiboutian flag represent the two
major groups of people who live there—blue for the Issas,
green for the Afars.

EGYPT (EE-jipt)
Capital: Cairo (KAI-roh). Population: 106.4 million.
Independence Day: July 23, 1952. Currency: Egyptian pound.

The Nile, the world's longest river, flows north from its most
distant source, the Kagera River in Burundi, for 4,132 miles
(6,650 km) to an immense delta in Egypt that empties into
the Mediterranean Sea.

EQUATORIAL GUINEA (GIH-nee)
Capital: Malabo (mah-LAH-boh).
Population: 857,000. Independence Day:
October 12, 1968. Currency: Central
African CFA franc.

Equatorial Guinea is the only country in Africa
that uses Spanish as a government language.

ERITREA (er-uh-TRAY-uh)
Capital: Asmara (az-MAHR-uh). Population: 6.1 million.
Independence Day: May 24,1993. Currency: nakfa.

When he was in school, Ghirmay Ghebreslassie's physical
education teacher in Eritrea suggested that he take up
running. In 2016, at the age of nineteen, Ghebreslassie
became the youngest male runner to win the New York
City Marathon and he placed fourth in the marathon in the
Olympic Games in Brazil.

ESWATINI (eh-SWAH-ti-nee)
Capital: Mbabane (uhm-bah-BAH-nay). Population:
1.1 million. Independence Day: September 6, 1968.
Currency: lilangeni.

Eswatini is ruled by a *ngwenyama*, a king. He is assisted by
a council of ministers and a legislature. The *ndlovukazi*, the
king's mother, is in charge of national rituals.

ETHIOPIA (ee-thee-OH-pee-uh)
Capital: Addis Ababa (ah-DEES AH-bah-bah). Population:
110.8 million. Patriots' Victory Day: May 5, 1941.
Currency: birr.

Ethiopia, which is at least two thousand years old, is the
oldest independent country in Africa, as it was never
colonized. Its flag dates back to the nineteenth century.
The colors on it, adopted from the 1950s through 1970s by
many other African countries upon independence (such as
Ghana, Mali, and Guinea-Bissau), have become known as
the Pan-African colors. Green symbolizes the fertility of
the land, red represents the struggle for independence, and
yellow stands for the sun, or mineral wealth.

GABON (gah-BOHN)
Capital: Libreville (LEE-bruh-veel). Population: 2.3 million.
Independence Day: August 17, 1960. Currency: Central
African CFA franc.

The majority of Gabonese live in cities and large towns.
The sparsely populated rain forest in the country's interior
is home to several varieties of elephants and more than
three thousand species of plants, among them the *okoume*, a
hardwood tree that is extensively logged.

GAMBIA (GAM-bee-uh)
Capital: Banjul (bahn-JOOL). Population: 2.2 million.
Independence Day: February 18, 1965. Currency: dalasi.

In order to write his best-selling book *Roots*, American author
Alex Haley traced his ancestry to the Gambia. He speculated
that he was a descendant of a Mandinka-speaking young man
who lived in Juffure before he was enslaved and shipped to
the American colonies in the late 1760s. Today Juffure is a
tourist attraction. Haley was awarded a special Pulitzer Prize
for his work in 1977.

GHANA (GAH-nuh)
Capital: Accra (AH-kruh). Population: 32.3 million.
Independence Day: March 6, 1957. Currency: cedi.

Children in Ghana know by heart folktales about Anansi, the
trickster spider. Anansi always seems to be in big trouble, but
often saves himself by using his head.

GUINEA (GIH-nee)
Capital: Conakry (KAH-nuh-kree). Population: 12.8 million.
Independence Day: October 2, 1958. Currency: Guinean
franc.

In the "bathing game," children face one another while sitting
on mounds of sand they have built in a circle at the beach. At
a signal, each player tries to land on the next mound. A player
is out if their feet touch the ground. The game continues until
one player is left.

GUINEA-BISSAU (GIH-nee bee-SOW)
Capital: Bissau. Population: 1.9 million. Independence Day:
September 24, 1973. Currency: West African CFA franc.

Amílcar Cabral was the key
leader in his country's struggle for
independence. An agronomist,
Cabral worked with farmers,
suggesting that they grow more than
peanuts, the major crop at that time.

KENYA (KEN-yuh)
Capital: Nairobi (nai-RO-bee).
Population: 54.6 million.
Independence Day: December 12,
1963. Currency: Kenyan shilling.

In 1977 Wangari Maathai started the Green Belt Movement
(GBM) in Nairobi, Kenya. She received the 2004 Nobel
Peace Prize in recognition of her work. Thanks to the GMB,
over fifty-one million trees have been planted across Kenya.
After Maathai's death in 2011, Africa Environment Day on
March 3 was changed to Wangari Maathai Day.

LESOTHO (leh-SOH-toh)
Capital: Maseru (MAH-say-roo). Population: 2.1 million.
Independence Day: October 4, 1966. Currency: loti.

Lesotho is surrounded on all sides by South Africa. The only
other two countries in the world that are encircled by a single
country are San Marino and Vatican City.

LIBERIA (lai-BEER-ee-uh)
Capital: Monrovia (muhn-RO-vee-uh). Population:
5.2 million. Independence Day: July 26, 1847. Currency:
Liberian dollar.

Monrovia was founded in 1822 by the American Colonization
Society, when formerly enslaved people from the United
States settled there. Liberia's name comes from *liber*, the
Latin word for "free."

LIBYA (LIH-bee-uh)
Capital: Tripoli (TRI-poh-lee). Population: 7 million.
Independence Day: December 24, 1951. Currency: Libyan
dinar.

One of the world's oldest-known instruments was played
about forty-five thousand years ago in what is now Libya.
Archaeologists unearthed a flute in a cave there, and after
extensive study they theorized that it was used not only to
entertain people but also to lure small animals to traps.

MADAGASCAR (ma-duh-GAS-kahr)
Capital: Antananarivo (ahn-tah-nah-nah-REE-voh).
Population: 27.5 million. Independence Day: June 26,1960.
Currency: Malagasy franc.

Hira Gasy is a weekly performance in or near the capital city
that blends dance, song, and speeches. Often young boys
perform acrobatic dances.

MALAWI (mah-LAH-wee)
Capital: Lilongwe (li-LONG-way). Population: 20.3 million.
Independence Day: July 6, 1964. Currency: kwacha.

One-fifth of Malawi's land is taken up by Lake
Malawi. Malawi's colonial name, Nyasaland,
means "land of the lake." Lake Malawi has over
one thousand distinct fish species—more than
any other lake in the world.

MALI (MAH-lee)
Capital: Bamako (BAH-mah-koh). Population:
20.1 million. Independence Day: September 22,
1960. Currency: West African CFA franc.

In 1905 the Grand Mosque, in Djenne, was
built with *banco*—sun-dried mud bricks. It is big enough
to hold three thousand worshippers. Every year rains wash
away its outer walls, but townspeople restore them during
the dry season.

MAURITANIA (maw-rih-TAY-nee-uh)
Capital: Nouakchott (noo-AHK-shaht). Population:
4.1 million. Independence Day: November 28, 1960.
Currency: ouguiya.

Mauritania's coastal waters are some
of the richest in the world. More
than 1 million tons (907,185 t) of
tuna, shrimp, and other fish are
caught in its waters each year.

38

**MAURITIUS** (maw-RIH-shyuhs)
Capital: Port Louis. Population: 1.3 million. Independence Day. March 12, 1968. Currency: Mauritian rupee.

In 1835 slavery was abolished on Mauritius. Indentured servants from India were brought in to work in the fields, and when their contracts expired, many of them decided to stay on the island. Today about two-thirds of the people who live in Mauritius are of Indian descent.

**MOROCCO** (muh-RAH-koh)
Capital: Rabat (rah-BAHT). Population: 36.5 million. Independence Day: March 2, 1956. Currency: dirham.

Men and women throughout Morocco often wear a jellaba when they are outdoors. This hooded robe with long sleeves is similar to the burnoose, a heavier robe that is worn by men, usually in rural areas.

**MOZAMBIQUE** (moh-zam-BEEK)
Capital: Maputo (mah-POO-toh). Population:30.8 million. Independence Day: June 25, 1975. Currency: Mozambique metical.

In the late 1400s and early 1500s, explorer Vasco da Gama sailed from Portugal to the coast of East Africa. He and his sailors were surprised by the wealth and knowledge of the people. From Mogadishu (now in Somalia) to Sofala (now in Mozambique), towns had been thriving for hundreds of years with an efficient trading system that stretched all the way to Asia.

**NAMIBIA** (nah-MIB-ee-uh)
Capital: Windhoek (VINT-huk). Population: 2.8 million. Independence Day: March 21, 1990. Currency: Namibian dollar.

Namib means "endless expanse" in the San language. Namibia's land is not thickly settled because it is one of the driest countries in the world.

**NIGER** (NAI-juhr)
Capital: Niamey (nee-AH-may). Population: 23.6 million. Independence Day: August 3, 1960. Currency: West African CFA franc.

Many elementary school students in Niger attend "maternal language" schools. Students not only learn their native language but are taught to honor and respect their culture.

**NIGERIA** (nai-JIR-ee-uh)
Capital: Abuja (ah-BOO-jah). Population: 219.4 million. Independence Day: October 1, 1960. Currency: naira.

Nigerian poet and novelist Chinua Achebe saw his book *Things Fall Apart* (1958) translated into more than forty languages. Wole Soyinka, a writer who was jailed from 1967 to 1969 for his political beliefs, won the Nobel Prize in Literature in 1986.

**RWANDA** (roo-WAHN-dah)
Capital: Kigali (kih-GAH-lee). Population: 12.9 million. Independence Day: July 1, 1962. Currency: Rwandan franc.

In Rwanda the last Saturday of every month is Umuganda. Able-bodied people between the ages of eighteen and sixty-five are required to work on community projects such as tree planting, farming, and house building. The word Umuganda can be translated as "coming together in common purpose to achieve an outcome."

**SÃO TOMÉ AND PRÍNCIPE** (sah-toh-MAY and PRIN-si-pee)
Capital: São Tomé. Population: 213,000. Independence Day: July 12, 1975. Currency: dobra.

In the early 1490s about two thousand Jewish children were forced to leave Portugal and were taken to São Tomé and Príncipe. The Portuguese wanted to populate the island and raise the children as Christians.

**SENEGAL** (seh-ni-GAHL)
Capital: Dakar (dah-KAHR. Population: 16.1 million. Independence Day: April 4, 1960. Currency: West African CFA franc.

Île de Gorée (Gorée Island) is 2 miles (3 km) from Dakar. Enslaved people were shipped there from all over West Africa in the 1600s and 1700s, then forced onto ships sailing to the Americas, never to return to their homes or families. Today Gorée Island is home to a museum called the Maison des Esclaves (House of Slaves).

**SEYCHELLES** (say-SHELZ)
Capital: Victoria. Population: 96,000. Independence Day: June 29, 1976. Currency: Seychelles rupee.

The Seychelles is home to the coco-de-mer (sea coconut). The fruit of this palm tree takes seven years to grow and weighs between 30 and 40 pounds (14 and 18 kg). Some of these coconuts float with the Indian Ocean currents to distant lands, where they are recovered and eaten.

**SIERRA LEONE** (see-EHR-ruh lee-OHN)
Capital: Freetown. Population 6.8 million. Independence Day: April 27, 1961. Currency: leone.

Freetown was founded by four hundred Black settlers who came from England in 1787. They were joined later by formerly enslaved people from Jamaica and Nova Scotia who had fought with the British during the US Revolutionary War. All told, several hundred thousand enslaved people, liberated by the British and others, eventually settled in Freetown.

SOMALIA (soh-MAH-lee-yah)
Capital: Mogadishu (moh-gah-DEE-shoo).
Population: 12.1 million. Independence
Day: July 1, 1960. Currency: Somali
shilling.

At birth, a child in Somalia is given not
only a personal name but also the name
of their father, their grandfather, their great-grandfather,
and his clan. However, since their names are so long, Somalis
rarely use all of them.

SOUTH AFRICA
Capital: Pretoria (prih-TAWR-ee-uh). Population: 56.9 million.
Freedom Day: April 27, 1994. Currency: rand.

In 1993 Nelson Mandela shared the Nobel Peace Prize with
then president F.W. de Klerk for their joint efforts to end
apartheid and to bring majority rule to South Africa.

SOUTH SUDAN (sowth soo-DAN)
Capital: Juba (JOO-buh). Population: 10.9 million.
Independence Day: July 9, 2011. Currency: South Sudanese
pound.

After decades of conflict, a referendum took place in January
2011 to determine whether an area of Sudan approximately
the size of Texas should become independent. Nearly
99 percent of the voting was in favor of independence, and
South Sudan officially became a country on July 9, 2011.

SUDAN (soo-DAN)
Capital: Khartoum (kahr-TOOM). Population: 46.8 million.
Independence Day: January 1, 1956. Currency: Sudanese
pound.

A Dinka boy in Sudan is given his first ox when he is twelve.
It is called his "song ox" because he is expected to compose a
song about it.

TANZANIA (tahn-zah-NEE-ah)
Capital: Dar es Salaam (dahr-es-sah-LAHM). Population:
62.1 million. Independence Day: December 9, 1961.
Currency: Tanzania shilling.

Serengeti, which means "endless plain" in the Maa language,
is the name of a wildlife park in Tanzania. This vast park,
which is larger than Connecticut, is one of 145 World
Heritage Sites in Africa. These areas were chosen by the
United Nations because of their cultural
and natural heritage.

TOGO (TOH-go)
Capital: Lomé (loh-MAY). Population:
8.2 million. Independence Day: April 27,
1960. Currency: West African CFA franc.

Two-story earthen homes, originally meant as protection
from attack, are built in northern Togo by the Batammaliba,
who are also called the Tamberma. The name Batammaliba
means "those who are the real architects of the earth."

TUNISIA (too-NEE-zhuh)
Capital: Tunis (TOO-nis). Population: 11.8 million.
Independence Day: March 20, 1956. Currency: Tunisian
dinar.

During the seventh century, when the Arab conquerors went
to the continent of Africa and what is now Tunisia, they
called it Ifriqiya. The word "Africa" is thought to be derived
from this. It may have also come from the word *afar*, an
Arabic word for "land," or it may be derived from *faraqa*, a
Carthaginian word meaning "colony."

UGANDA (yoo-GAHN-dah)
Capital: Kampala (kahm-PAH-lah). Population: 44.7 million.
Independence Day: October 9, 1962.
Currency: Ugandan shilling.

Lake Victoria is the world's
second-largest freshwater lake (only
Lake Superior is bigger), covering
one-sixth of Uganda and parts of
Kenya and Tanzania. An estimated five
hundred species of cichlid fish live in it.

WESTERN SAHARA
Capital: Laâyoune (lah-YOON). Population: 567,000.
Independence Day: not applicable. Currency: Moroccan
dirham.

Though controlled by Morocco since 1979, and therefore
not yet an independent nation, Western Sahara is sometimes
counted as Africa's fifty-fifth country. Using self-government
as the criteria for nationhood, we refer to fifty-four African
countries on page 3, though the map shows the border
between Western Sahara and Morocco.

ZAMBIA (ZAM-bee-ah)
Capital: Lusaka (loo-SAH-kah). Population: 19 million.
Independence Day: October 24, 1964. Currency: kwacha.

Mosi-oa-Tunya, which means "smoke that thunders" in the
Lozi and Kololo languages, is also known as Victoria Falls.
The world's largest sheet of falling water, the falls are on the
Zambezi River, which forms the border between Zambia
and Zimbabwe.

ZIMBABWE (zim-BAHB-way)
Capital: Harare (hah-RAH-ray). Population: 14.8 million.
Independence Day: April 18, 1980. Currency: Zimbabwean
dollar.

Though now uninhabited, the stone walls of Great
Zimbabwean still stand. These ruins are visited by people
from all over the world as a way to learn firsthand about
Shona history.

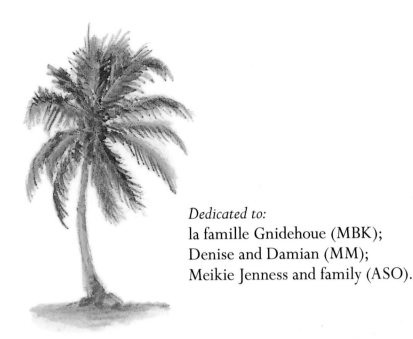

*Dedicated to:*
la famille Gnidehoue (MBK);
Denise and Damian (MM);
Meikie Jenness and family (ASO).

ACKNOWLEDGMENTS:

With deep appreciation to all those who shared their expertise and stories of African childhoods:

Naa Anorkor Abbey-Baurecht, Simeon Alloding, Mohamed and Radia Gheraissa, Ahmed Hassan, Sylvanus Jackson, Meikie Jenness, Nancy Kamaliza, E'nkul Kanakan, Margaret Lado, Metycaine Mntuyedwa and family, Oscar Mokeme, Penjami Mphepo, Apollinaire Munyaneza, Thandi Nkosi, Brigitte Nyada and family, Mutima Peter, Efrem Weldemichael, Kokou Yetongnon, Catherine Yomoah, and Aster Zaoude.

To Edgard Gnidehoue for his guidance, to Daria Burns for her research assistance, and to Barbara Brown for her knowledge.

And to all those who helped us along the way: The African Studies Center at Boston University (Africa@bu.edu), Charlotte Agell, Dale Barrett, Bates College, Mara Burns, Toni Buzzeo, Jo Coyne, Meri Nana-Ama Danquah, Mirjam de Bruijn, DeWolfe Family, Mansour El-Alwi, Paul Fredrick, Val Hart, Jay Hoffman, Emilie Knight, Steve Knight, Jane Kurtz, Agnes Leslie, Ann Lynch, Marguerite MacDonald, the McPhedran Family, Cathy Murray, Marcia Nash, Katie Norton, Robert O'Brien, Yunhee O'Brien, Melissa Orth, Pam Osborn, George Packer, the Peace Corps, Jim Perkins, Portland Public Library and Peaks Island Branch, the Reinsboroughs, John and Jean Sibley, Norman R. Sibley, Peg Snyder, Carol Stahl, Pat Stanton, Elizabeth Stover, Rachel Talbot-Ross, UM-Orono, Grace Valenzuela, Gretchen Walsh, Dianne Webb, Cathy Wimette, Winthrop Grade School, and Winthrop High School French IV class.

Although every effort has been made to make this book as accurate as possible, some facts are in dispute, even by experts. The diversity, complexity, and changing nature of the African continent means that new information is always arising.

Millbrook Press™
An imprint of Lerner Publishing Group, Inc.
241 First Avenue North
Minneapolis, MN 55401 USA

For reading levels and more information, look up this title at www.lernerbooks.com.

Main body text set in Perpetua Std. Typeface provided by Monotype Typography.

**Library of Congress Cataloging-in-Publication Data**

Names: Knight, Margy Burns, author. | Melnicove, Mark, author. | O'Brien, Anne Sibley, illustrator.
Title: Africa is not a country / Margy Burns Knight, Mark Melnicove ; illustrated by Anne Sibley O'Brien.
Description: 2nd edition. | Minneapolis : Millbrook Press, [2022] | Audience: Ages 8–12 | Audience: Grades 4–6 | Summary: "Enter into the daily lives of children in the many countries of modern Africa. Countering stereotypes, this book celebrates the extraordinary diversity of this vibrant continent. With selected updates to the text, statistics, and illustrations" —Provided by publisher.
Identifiers: LCCN 2021052296 | ISBN 9781728460383 (library binding) | ISBN 9781728460390 (paperback) | ISBN 9781728462653 (ebook pdf)
Subjects: LCSH: Africa—Juvenile literature. | Africa—Social life and customs—Juvenile literature.
Classification: LCC DT22 .K57 2022 | DDC 960—dc23/eng/20211106

LC record available att https://lccn.loc.gov/2021052296

Manufactured in the United States of America
1-51506-50378-1/27/2022